FL;P

Finding Love In Purpose

BRITTANY N. BROOKS

The events portrayed in this book are relayed to the best of Brittany's memory. While all the stories in the book are true, some names have been changed to protect the privacy of individuals involved.

None of the information presented is done with the intent of defaming any individual person.

FL;P

A Healing Guide To

Find Love In Purpose

After A Heartbreak

"Oh yes, you shaped me first inside, then out;
you formed me in my mother's womb.
I thank you, High God—you're breathtaking!
Body and soul, I am marvelously made!
I worship in adoration—what a creation!
You know me inside and out,
you know every bone in my body;
You know exactly how I was made, bit by bit,
how I was sculpted from nothing into something.
Like an open book, you watched me grow from conception to birth; all
the stages of my life were spread out before you,
The days of my life all prepared
before I'd even lived one day.
Your thoughts—how rare, how beautiful!
God, I'll never comprehend them!
I couldn't even begin to count them—
any more than I could count the sand of the sea.
Oh, let me rise in the morning and live always with you!"

Psalm 139:13-18 MSG

DEDICATION

"Now faith is the substance of things hoped for, the evidence of things not seen." Hebrews 11:1 KJV

This book is lovingly dedicated to my brother, Lowell T. Brooks II, affectionately known as LJ. Thank you for teaching me how to be strong and to push through every circumstance. Thank you for being my biggest supporter. Thank you for being my listening ear through every heartbreak. Thank you for being my eyes when I couldn't see my own beauty. Thank you for guiding me through this journey I call purpose. You are the greatest faith fighter I know. I admire your strength, your faith, your ambition, your tenacity, your vision, your passion, your leadership, and how you enjoyed life to the fullest. LJ, you have taught me to go after my passions and to pursue my purpose with my whole heart. I miss you deeply and words cannot express how much I wish you were here. I know heaven has gained an incredible soul. Your life and the memories we shared for 27 years will never fade from my heart. You will forever be my rock, my heartbeat, my song.

Until we meet again my love.

With All My Heart,

Your Sissy

CONTENTS

INTRODUCTION

"Watch for the new thing I am going to do. It is happening already—you can see it now! I will make a road through the wilderness and give you streams of water there."
Isaiah 43:19 GNT

I don't believe you picked up this book by coincidence. I believe you picked up this book by divine appointment. Maybe you just got out of a dysfunctional relationship and are trying to figure out what's next for you and your life? Maybe you're in a broken relationship and you don't have the strength to free yourself. Maybe you're not in relationship, but you're fed up with being the "2am girl." Or, could it be that you're sick and tired of finding love in all the wrong people. Whatever your reason may be, you have been led to this book.

Like many people, you have been searching for purpose and fulfillment in love. You long for a healing in your heart, and you've looked for it in every high and low place. Yet, still...you feel incomplete. For too long, your heart, mind, body, and soul have been running on empty. You've invested in relationships hoping they would fill a void, but still, you feel hollow. You've given your heart to people hoping to gain their love, only to find, in the end, your self-worth, ingenuity, and purpose depleted. Time and time again, you've lost your identity and put aside your values to keep a relationship. You look in the mirror every day and ask yourself, "What am I?" "Who am I?" "Why does this keep happening to me?" and "What am I doing wrong?"

There were times in my life that I found myself asking these same questions. Finally, I came to realize that it's hard to find yourself, when you don't know yourself. It's hard to love yourself, when you give away parts of yourself to so many people. Like many of you, I spent countless sleepless nights struggling with the question, "God, will my heart ever recover from what I have been through?"

Again, is a common theme for people like us. "I am tired of being hurt...*again.*" "I am tired of being used...*again.*" "I am tired of giving my heart away, only to have it crushed...*again.*" "Will I ever find love...*again?*" I found myself making these statements after every relationship ended.

Sound familiar?

POUR MY LOVE ON YOU

I was sitting on the edge of my bed. Juanita Bynum's song *Pour My Love On You* was playing in the background. Tissues fell one-by-one out of my hands to the edge of the bed, and then down to the floor. The dark craters under my eyes were evidence of the lack of sleep I got that night. It felt as if 500 pound weights were chained to and hanging on my heart and mind. I hugged my pillow tight as the tears rolled down my face. I felt broken, empty, and confused. "Why me?" I asked myself. This was the fourth guy who had cheated on me. "Why do I keep attracting these selfish guys?" "Why do I put myself through this?" It was as if I had a sign on my forehead that read, "Hey, I like to be used and I don't care if you cheat on me!" I was the poster child for selfless love. I had so much love to give, but, I was too naive to know that I needed to guard my most precious jewel...my heart.

And now, just like the other guys, he had taken my kindness for weakness. If he needed money, clothes, or shoes, without hesitation, I gave them to him. If he needed food, I was at the nearest grocery store or restaurant buying it for him. Gas for his car? "Take my card, I got you," I'd say. You name the circumstance, I was there for him. I invested everything into this guy, money, time, and love, but he didn't care to love me.

When I finally decided to stop giving, it became clear he was only with me for what I could offer him financially and physically. My free heartedness had left me spiritually, emotionally, mentally, and physically bankrupt in the end. As long as I was giving him what he wanted, I was his prized trophy. "The best woman in the world," he would say.

Sometimes, it seems like being his trophy is a good thing. But in truth, it is just a misconception of affection.

I was blind. As long as he was parading me around his so-called friends, I was convinced that it was true love. I couldn't see that he was infecting me with so many lies. Like most unattended trophies, after he won me over, I stayed on the shelf and accumulated dust. He never took the time to notice me again. I became his afterthought.

After two years, the relationship ended and I fell into a deep depression. After we broke up, I couldn't manage to recover. My heart was searching for the right path, to find what was next for my life, but I was stuck. I stayed in my room, living in the midst of a silent storm, hiding the fact that I was struggling from my family and friends. I was so ashamed of my bad choice in men, especially this guy, and the mistakes I had made as I dated him. I didn't know who to turn to for help. I feared being judged and stereotyped for my decision to stay with him.

If only they understood that I did it out of love or, so I thought at the time. I repeatedly berated myself realizing, in the end, that I had focused on a man and neglected my purpose. I had put his career, his aspirations, his needs before my own. I didn't even know what my purpose was, and I had no idea what steps to take to find it.

It's impossible to find your purpose in life when you have never defined it. When we get involved in relationships, but we don't know our own purpose, we often expect our partner to define it for us. We jump from one relationship to the next wondering, "Is this person my purpose?"

I want to be candid in this book. The truth is, I struggled with finding my purpose for years and I often sought to find it in my relationships. I wanted so badly to be accepted and loved by men. I lived my life feeling there was something that I lacked, and I thought having a man would help me find what I needed. I wanted to be accepted and loved so badly that I did unhealthy things to my heart, my mind, and my body. I even put myself in some abusive circumstances, just so I wouldn't be alone.

There were times when I was cursed out, belittled, and screamed at, I even had things thrown at me. And each time, I would suppressed my pain into what I call a *cover girl*. A *cover girl* is a woman who pretends to be okay on the outside, but, in truth, her spirit is dying on the inside. I thought being with someone, even someone who treated me badly, was better than being by myself. I accepted whatever treatment I had to take to get what I mistakenly defined as my purpose, as love, to avoid being alone.

This pattern of behavior led to depression, guilt, insecurity, unworthiness, resentment, confusion, and bitterness. But there was hope for me, and, if you are reading this and recognize yourself in my story, there is hope for you too.

Scripture says, "Instead of shame and dishonor, you will enjoy a double share of honor. You will possess a double portion of prosperity in your land, and everlasting joy will be yours" (Isaiah 61:7 NLT). As *Pour My Love On You* continued to play in the background of my room, I whispered to God,

"Please heal me. I'm tired of these cycles." In that second, it felt like a sweet, soft peace entered into my room. I could feel God's peace surrounding my bed. I could feel his gentle hands touch my broken heart.

God began to minister affirmations to me, reminding me that I didn't have to be ashamed of my past mistakes or choices. He was making sure I knew that my heart would recover and there was no condemnation in Him. He let me know that which was broken (my heart, mind, emotions, and body), He was able to restore it. After enduring years of pain, relationship after relationship, I entrusted God to be the keeper of my heart. I stopped asking, "God why can't I find my purpose?" And instead, started asking Him to *teach me my purpose.* I lifted my head from my pillow, wiped my face and sat up on the bed. "It seems like no one wants me, God, what is it that You want from me?" I heard His answer very clearly. "I want your heart," He said. "Allow me to heal your heart and help you find love in your purpose. As I heal you, I will also give you the gift of letting go of your painful past. No longer shall you walk in condemnation, fear, guilt, or shame. But you shall walk in this confidence, to be true to thyself is to love thyself." Like the song, God poured His unconditional love on me. He turned my ashes into a beautiful love story.

FINDING LOVE IN PURPOSE

F L ; P, *Finding Love In Purpose*, is a chance for you to discover you. It's a timeout from searching to find yet another relationship, and instead a time to develop a relationship with yourself. This book is a roadmap that will guide you through what have likely been some of the darkest valleys of your past and your pain. Together, we will cast out the old, throw away the masks we wear to hide our true selves, and purge every insecurity. Together, we are going to heal God's way, from the inside out.

F L ; P is not just a self-help book, but it is a healing beyond what your eyes can see. Have you ever been in a relationship where you lost yourself? Where the hurt was so deeply locked in the cages of your heart that you felt you were damaged goods and not worthy of a recovery? Let me be the first to sign up on that list. I've been abandoned, rejected, mistreated, and oftentimes abused in relationships. And due to those deep wounds and scars from that hurt, much like you, I was ready to give up on happiness. I was ready to give up on love. I was ready to give up on my purpose. I was ready to give up on what God had destined for my life. I was so focused on the pain I felt and the mistakes of my past, that I couldn't see the plot twist that God was creating for my life. There were many times when I said, "love is not for me" and "purpose will never find its way to my heart."

Throughout this book, I will share stories of how my life's battles tried to put a period behind my pain and keep me in the state of brokenness. I will share how my messes tried to put a period behind my shame and keep me bound from sharing the message of redemption. In fact, there were points in my life where my heart hit rock bottom and I knew this was my end all be all. However, God saw otherwise. God was not done with me yet and He is not done with you either. Just because that man or woman is finished with you, doesn't mean God has ended His relationship with you. He never neglects his children. He never lets you lose to life, but He does teach you how to gain. Just by picking up this book, He has already begun to do a new work in you. The question is, will you let Him complete it?

Don't be embarrassed, I too, struggled with the back and forth of making the right decision to stay or to leave unhealthy relationships. Deep down, I longed for a true, untainted love. A love that was filled with happiness; however, on the surface level I continued to settle for unhappiness.

When relationships or "situationships" are not working in our favor, we tend to place periods after our hurt. However, God is saying *that's not the end for you.* God is saying, "Do you really think that's all I have for you? Do you really think I am going to leave you to settle in brokenness?" Absolutely, not! But we often settle into hopelessness, rather than making a change to live in the hope He has created for us. When relationships don't go our way, we will channel feelings such as:

There is no hope.
There is nothing left.
I am broken.
I will never experience love.

But, our God says...

When there is no hope; I am the giver of hope.
When there is nothing left; behold, I am creating a new thing.
When you are broken; I am the restorer of the broken heart.
When you think you will never experience love; I am pouring my love
on you unconditionally.

Basically, He is telling you, *this is not the end my sons and daughters*! He's letting you know there's another part of life that you have not discovered. Not only will God give you something new, but He will take those wounds, those scars, those broken pieces, and heal you completely.

I will tell you from experience, this healing journey will not be easy. We will laugh, but we will cry too. We will take this walk and get through this together, and, in the end, arrive at a beautiful reward...hope.

Whether you are a woman or a man, I encourage you to open your heart and mind to what you read on the pages of this book. We will tear down walls and break all forms of ego, judgements, and pride. In each chapter, I will share my personal stories of struggles, how I overcame them, how I learned to find my strength, how I learned to love myself, and how to avoid reversing my recovery by making the same mistakes again. And, if you find yourself wanting to leave an unpromising relationship, or you already have, I pray that my stories will give you the courage to embark on your own journey of healing so that you too can find your life's purpose and learn to love yourself as God does.

As you read each chapter, I pray you grab a hold of God's healing message, and that you will find hope in Him. God gives hope to the lost and He is a Redeemer of the broken. I sincerely hope that you establish a new relationship in God and are renewed in Him as I have been. I pray that your confidence and your power will be restored. I pray that God will mend your broken heart, renew your mind, and place in you a sense of purpose and hope for your life.

In all, as I was healed, I want you to be healed. As I feel free, I want you to be free. As I was delivered, I want you to be delivered. I know it is possible because He did it for me.

Shall we begin?

Part I

What does it mean to **F.I.N.D.**?

In this section, you will learn how to "**Funnel** your **Inspiration and Nourish** your **Destiny**." It hurts to lose a relationship. It hurts even more to lose yourself, your power, your inspiration, and your motivation to continue on in life. People often ask me what tools they can use to help find who they are and what they want? This section will teach you how to find the inspiration you need to begin to pursue your purpose and discover the real you. It will also give you the tools on how to nourish your destiny. Remember with every healing journey, God will never leave you *empty handed*. He will always equip you and prepare you for what is coming next.

1

CHANGE YOUR ANTHEM

"Words satisfy the mind as much as fruit does the stomach; good talk is as gratifying as a good harvest. Words kill, words give life; they're either poison or fruit - you choose."
Proverbs 18:20-21 MSG

So, here I was again...back to square one, back to being single. At some point in our lives, most of us have experienced a breakup. Whether it was a situationship that ended or a love relationship gone wrong, I think we can all agree that breakups can be devastating. We may put on our happy face mask and act as if everything is "peachy and dreamy." But, let's be real. While there may be some days when we feel like we're on top of the mountain, there are likely more days that we feel in the lowest valley. Undeniably, staying on top of the mountain is usually fleeting. Heartbreak valley is where we often choose to live.

2

Heartbreak valley is not a real place, it lives in our mind. It's dirty and contaminated with hurtful memories of those bad past relationships. In heartbreak valley, the regrets, the guilt, and the shame of being with the wrong person play over and over in our minds like a bad movie.

The valley has a cunning side too. Have you ever found yourself reminiscing about the good ole days? Those early, exciting, blissful days when everything was new and before everything went downhill? Heartbreak valley likes to play with our emotions and make us believe that we need those days back, or worse that we'll never have happy days with the right person.

As I've worked to heal and overcome the pain of my bad relationships, what I learned from my own experiences, and from speaking to others, is that we subject ourselves to these thoughts because it's hard to escape the memories of bad decisions, and what we allowed someone to do to us. The thoughts of being used, abused, betrayed, abandoned, cheated on, mistreated, disappointed, rejected, or neglected play on repeat in our heads.

In all, we wasted our time! And on some level, most times, we knew we were doing it. In heartbreak valley we continue to search for *the why* in what they have done. We demand answers. We demand clarity. We demand closure. We demand the truth.

Truth is, it is hard to let go of an investment, someone you have spent so much time, money, energy, tears, and even laughs with. In my own experiences, I found that I often didn't want to let go of relationships because of my pride. I didn't want the next woman to benefit from all of the time and effort I invested in the relationship. I was afraid she would not have to commit as hard as I did. In fact, because of my pride, I felt she might be loved and treated better than me! I will admit, I went back into relationships for that reason.

MOONWALK

We were on and off for two years up until the day he confessed that he was cheating. He had called me at work. "Are you serious right now?" I said, as I tried to maintain my composure so my co-workers wouldn't hear me. I gripped the phone, pressing it to my ear, listening as he explained in detail who she was and how long they'd been seeing each other. A very private person, I was not in the habit of having such a personal discussion at work. Before he could say sorry, I hung up the phone.

I decided to take an early lunch, not because I was hungry, but because I was desperate to run away from this nightmare. I drove to a nearby shopping center, just around the corner from the office building where I worked and parked my car. My body felt numb. My hands were ice cold. My heart felt as heavy as a wet, wool, winter coat.

I sat there, crying so hard that the charcoal colored mascara I had put on that morning flowed like rivers through the rosey blush on my cheeks. I felt dead inside. I was in shock and it felt hard to breathe.

I banged my fists on the car windows and the steering wheel, shouting "I was good to him! Why did he have to do this to me! I wish I never met him! I hate him!"

A barrage of negative thoughts ran through my mind. I had wasted my time. I saw the signs, but refused to pay attention. I felt ugly as a person. I felt betrayed. I felt useless, worthless, and utterly confused. I felt like I wasn't good enough for anyone. I vowed to myself that it was over and that I would never go back to him. "This is it! It's his loss." I laid my head back on the head rest and stared out the window at nothing in particular. "Please, help me," I desperately whispered to God, "If you save me from this pain, I promise, I won't go back to him."

My cell phone rang and interrupted my prayer. It was him. I sat there staring at the familiar name and number on the screen. "Be strong," I said to myself. I was sure there was nothing he could say or do to convince me to take him back. I pressed the *ignore call* button and sent him to voicemail.

Moments later the phone rang a second time, then a third, and a fourth. When calling didn't work, he began to text me. *Pick up the phone. I love you. Why are you ignoring me?* The bell indicating a new message chimed over and over. *Ding, ding, ding.* I was determined to stand firm. But, you know how it works. Why is that once you make up your mind that you are done with a toxic relationship, that person comes back even harder? And that's exactly what happened. *I will call you one more time* said the text *and if you don't pick up the phone, then I will leave you alone forever.* And then, the phone rang.

I wanted to hate him, but I couldn't. I wanted him to disappear, but he didn't. I loved him, or at least I thought I did. And that misguided idea of love made me answer the phone. I held it to my ear without speaking. His voice was shaky as if he'd been crying, "Brittany are you there? Look, you don't have to say a word. I know you are angry and you have every right to be." He explained, "It was my mistake. I never loved her. I only want you...I am sorry. Please, stay. Don't leave me. I'll change for you. Where are you? I want to see you."

He was caught and he knew it, and he said all the right things. Deep down inside I heard my inner angel saying, "Don't go back to him. He's lying to you, he will never change." And although I knew that they were fallen words, I accepted his lies anyway. "Okay," I said, "I forgive you."

We moonwalk, knowing they will never change. I couldn't imagine my future with another man. We had history. I felt like he was the only man that accepted me and my flaws. There was no way I was letting all of that wash away. I was a forgiving person and so I moonwalked back to him. I believe everyone should get another chance, regardless of how many mistakes they've made. And, I stayed with him because I didn't want to be a quitter in the relationship. I've never quit anything, no matter how hard it was.

My pride superseded my tolerance for pain. Rather than letting go, I found myself enduring more heartache, just so some other woman wouldn't reap what I had sown. Although his cheating cycles continued, I moonwalked because I didn't want to be alone.

We dread being alone, don't we? We stay in heartbreak valley because we believe we cannot function by ourselves. Oftentimes, when you leave a relationship, it is hard to go places without thinking about them. And, it is difficult to enjoy the beauty of life and to pursue your own purpose, because your calendar was always centered around them. Without them, you feel like you know nothing, including yourself.

Living in heartbreak valley keeps your freedom and purpose chained to the past. You wonder how to escape the pain and the memories of the relationship. When you find yourself in heartbreak valley you have two choices. You can stay, give up hope, and choose not to heal. Or, you can choose to press forward. When we lock ourselves to the past rather than move on, we fail to embrace what the future has to offer us.

You will wonder, "Will I ever get over him/her quickly?" "Will my heart ever be the same?" The answer is *no*! If I said yes, I would be lying to you. Word of advice, a healing heart takes time. Your heart will never be the same, but your heart will be better. The only way your heart can get better, the only way to get over the pain of your past, is to allow yourself the time and space you need to heal. Healing is critical when it comes to the pursuit of your purpose. Without healing you will continue to repeat past mistakes and experience depression, hopelessness, bitterness, and anger. By staying tied to the past, eventually, you will overpower your life anthem.

YOUR LIFE'S ANTHEM

A life anthem is your own song, filled with words of life, healing, devotion, and love. A life anthem is a declaration that proclaims your purpose and affirms the greatness that is within you.

For instance, whenever I thought about the past hurts of my relationship, I would sing my life anthem. It brought life back to me. It reminded me that *I can and will make it!* However, I've watched people become so focused on negative anthems that, rather than lifting them up, they overpowered their recovery. Instead of singing the song of "I am worth the wait!" Instead of singing the song of "I am fearfully and wonderfully made!" We instead choose to sing anthems like:

"Maybe, I'm not good enough."

"Maybe, I deserve to be hurt."

"Maybe, it's my fault he/she cheated."

"Maybe, I deserve to be unhappy."

"Maybe, relationships are not meant for me."

The Bible speaks of the power of the tongue, how our words can bring death or life to our situation. My parents always taught me to guard my mind, my words, my heart, and my body. Have I always? No. I have made many mistakes and wish I could undo them - especially when it came to my choice in relationships.

But the key word here is, my *choice*. I don't say this to beat myself up, or to beat you up. We are not here to place blame. But, we have to be honest with ourselves about our repeated patterns and our contributions to our circumstances. When I invested the time to reflect on my past experiences and the resulting lessons, my mind was opened to a new understanding about the importance of changing my anthem.

Here are five key reflections I arrived at:

1) *The only way to overcome a heartbreak is by changing your anthem.* Words have power. Words have significance. Words have an impact. The right words have healing. What you say will either make you or break you. What you say will either push you forward or pull you back. What you say will either heal you or destroy you. Choose the lyrics to your life anthem wisely.

2) *Stop playing the anthems of bitterness, resentment and unforgiveness.* Do not allow bitterness, resentment, and unforgiveness to infiltrate your mind and your heart. You have to forgive those that have hurt you. You have to forgive yourself. You do not want to carry the heavy bags of unforgiveness, bitterness, and resentment into your destiny. Why? It will be a hindrance to the purpose

God has for you and the next relationship God is preparing you for. It's time to play a new life anthem called hope!

3) *Despite all that you have been through - your anthem should be a replica of grace.* When people look at you, they should see the grace of God. It is by His grace that you know better is ahead. It is by His grace that you know it was God who brought you out of darkness. It is by His grace that you know you were not overtaken by your past. It is by His grace that you are overcome by the word of your testimony.

4) *Your anthem must be clear and direct.* Scripture says, "Write the vision, and make it plain upon tables" (Habakkuk 2:2 KJV). It is important that you be specific about what you desire for your life. You have to not only write your vision, but you also have to live in what you say. You have probably heard the saying, "Don't just talk the talk, but walk the walk." When I finally decided to make a change in my life, one of the things that I wrote down was, *I will love and value myself. I will no longer settle for less, but will obtain God's best. I will live for me and not through the opinions of others.* Then in life, I had to stay true to my anthem. If I said, "I will not settle for less," then I couldn't subject myself to counterfeit men. Counterfeit men pretend to value you, but are sent to distract you from your purpose. Ladies, I could not put a crown on a counterfeit and expect a king. A queen can

never build a kingdom with a man who still craves pleasure from the village. If I said, *I love myself and I will value myself,* then I couldn't put my heart and body in undeserving, malnourished relationships. It is important that you live by your anthem.

5) *Have you ever tried to find love in people and pain?* Have you ever felt like you have exhausted all of your options? But, have you tried His option? Did you know that God has given you an expected beautiful end? When you decided to add a period to your painful situation, He decided to add a comma underneath to signify that your purpose has not ended. In fact, He has flipped it and created another way for you. I encourage you to let God be the ghostwriter of your anthem. Where man tried to put an end to your purpose, God is saying let me write your F L ; P anthem. In His lyrics, He is saying that:

> *This is not the end for my son or daughter! There's another part of life that you have not discovered. Not only will I give you something new, but allow me to take those wounds, those scars, those broken pieces, and let me heal you.*

Let me be frank, it's easy to control someone who sees herself or himself as a victim of pain, but it is not easy to control a healed person. As an evolved, healed woman, I'm not interested in pain. I'm interested in purpose and who God has called me to be. I'm not interested in placing periods after my pain. Yet, I will let God place a semi-colon on my heart because I recognize that He is not finished with me yet.

I encourage you to use my five revelations to kickstart your quest to find your own purpose. It's time out for the *woe is me* anthem and time in for the *wow, it's me* anthem! You have the power to change your life. You are in control of what and who enters, and what and who exits. It's time to allow the healing, the love, and the joy to enter into your heart. It's time to kick out the bitterness, the unforgiveness, the pride, the moonwalk mindset, and the heartbreak valleys. I believe in you. I believe in your purpose. I believe in your life anthem. It's time to believe in yourself.

PRAY ON PURPOSE

Heavenly Father, I recognize that the first step to finding love in my own purpose is to change my anthem. God, I want you to change my anthem from the inside and allow it to reflect on the outside. For too long, I have sung the anthem of self-pity, rejection, resentment, guilt, unworthiness, and fear. You did not create me to be empty. You did not create me to be insecure, but you created me for a purpose. Father, show me that purpose. Change my anthem that reflects the beauty of how You see me. Change my anthem that reflects the greatness You see in me. Change my anthem that reflects the worth and value You have created for me to be. In Jesus' name, Amen.

2

FINDING THE WORD

"By your words I can see where I'm going; they throw a beam of light on my dark path." Psalm 119:105 MSG

She walked confidently up to the microphone on the pulpit, hands were clapping, feet were stomping, and the sound of praise filled the sanctuary. "Let's give God a shout! Our God is a Wonderful Counselor! Our God is a Friend like no other! Our God is a Healer!" But little did the congregation know, that behind the mic, stood a broken woman. A woman who was carrying with her the verbal abuse from the night before. On the outside she looked strong, whole, and confident. However, the woman's self-esteem was so low it was on the brink of empty. Her heart felt like it was bleeding.

That woman was me.

Looking at me you would never have a clue. Growing up in church, I quickly learned how to put on my Sunday best, with my favorite navy blue dress, pearl white blazer, nude heels, and Kate Spade accessories. I looked the part of the perfect "church girl." I knew how to look good on the outside and to coat the pain I felt inside. My *Amen* and *Hallelujah* were always on cue. I had mastered the art of the church cover up. I could take the ugly feelings I had about myself and my relationship and cover them over with the perfect church outfit. I was what I like to call the perfect *cover girl*.

I pose this question to the ladies, "Have you ever been a *cover girl* in a relationship?" A woman who pretends to be okay on the outside, but her spirit is dying on the inside. A *cover girl* is an expert at concealing her pain. She knows what outfits to wear to cover the scars of brokenness. She knows what makeup to wear to hide the unworthiness on her face. She knows what concealers to choose to cover the blemishes in the relationship. She knows what shadows and mascaras will brush away the truth in her eyes. She dresses her lips in the perfect color to keep from speaking the truth.

I was his *cover girl*. I pretended that our relationship was happy and full of love. I pretended that he treated me like a queen. I pretended that he was faithful. That was my daily *cover girl* routine. Soon his lies became my lies. I would advocate for him, defend him, even though I knew the truth.

The truth was, he was cheating. The truth was, he was mentally and verbally abusive. The truth was, I refused to allow

God to set me free. People would ask, "How are you two doing?" But before I could answer, the *cover girl* inside me would blurt out lies, "We're good. Everything is wonderful." I would even add a smile to be sure I suppressed my heartache. I used these *cover girl* tactics to save myself the embarrassment of admitting what was really happening, and to convince the spectators that my relationship was perfect. But, nothing was further from the truth. The fact was, the relationship was destructive.

My true identity was fading on the inside, and sadly, I knew it. My passion for the things of God were slowly depleting. I was reading the Word less, praying less, fasting less, and seeking God less. I was emotionally consumed with trying to please a man that did not love me. I was too focused on securing a commitment with him rather than securing my purpose. The people close to me, my friends, and my family, knew it. My family offered help, but I refused it. I didn't want to hear, "I told you so!" I didn't want to listen to the sound wisdom of my loved ones. I allowed my pride to clog my ears and I stayed in the relationship. The longer I stayed, the more I lost my identity.

Have you ever lost your self-worth for the sake of making it work? I admit, I have stayed in bad relationships that cost me my purpose. I can reflect on the times where I put the guy above my own needs. In other times, I put him and our relationship before God. The personal time I had set aside for God, was now spent on the guy. There were times where I could be reading a devotional or praying, but as soon as he called, I would put God on hold to answer his call. At other times, I could be working on my purpose, for example, writing my book or developing a business plan. But if he would text, *You busy?* I would put my purpose on hold and make myself available for him. My selfish actions showed that he was more important than God and more important than the plan God had for my life. Day after day, I found myself communicating less with God and focusing more on the guy. The standards that I grew to live by: *to keep God first and to always love myself,* had faded away.

When we do not value ourselves, we expect others to give us that value. When we do not value ourselves, often, we will attract someone even more broken and damaged than we are. We think we can make each other whole, when in fact we are wounding each other. Yes, this relationship was rushed. Yes, we were broken. Yes, we thought we could be each other's "saving grace." However, our past guilt and insecurities were only just digging deeper holes for each other. We were stuck in the past and eventually buried each other and our purposes.

I AM NOT A COVER GIRL

Finally, enough was enough! I realized I needed to make a serious soul change in my life. We were both attending a Super Bowl party at a friend's house. As much as I love the game of football, Super Bowl commercials, good food, and company, I felt despondent that night. I decided to leave before halftime. On my way home, I cried out to God to rescue my broken heart. I told Him that I was tired of living a lie just to please the people who wanted us to be together. I was tired of pretending that the love he was giving me was well deserving, when in fact it was tormenting. I needed God to deliver my heart from this ugly pit. I could not wait another day, another week, or a month. I needed God to do the 180 in my life now!

You ask, how do you get yourself out of a situation like this? First, I had to remove the *cover girl* mask I was wearing. By removing this mask, I was declaring that I was breaking every emotional soul tie that kept me bound to him. I was declaring that I loved myself and my heart belonged in the hands of God and not with this man. I was declaring that from this day forward I would be true to myself. I was declaring that I was not his *cover girl,* but I was God's girl.

My makeup users can attest to this, too much makeup can lead to too much buildup inside the pores. Can you imagine how my face looked after three years? This *cover girl* was in need of a spiritual facial, with all the works.

I walked in the house and went straight to my nightstand and pulled out my Bible from the top drawer. I sank into the chair in the corner of my room and opened it. There staring at me from the page was Psalm 34:6, "This poor man cried, and the Lord heard him, and saved him out of all his troubles."

It is amazing how God's Word will perform a search and rescue on your heart. I let the Word of God become my *cover girl* mask remover. The more I read, the more the Word began to purge out every blemish of hurt, rejection, and shame. The Word began to tear down walls I never knew I had. It was His Word that changed me. It was His Word that brought me into alignment with my true identity and purpose. It was His Word that brought me back in communion with Him. It was His Word that helped me wash away the old *cover girl* and build a new foundation on His love.

This was not an overnight process. In order to experience that change within, I had to commit myself to reading the Word daily. I set aside special devotion time with God, 15 minutes every day, when I got up in the morning and before I went to bed in the evening. Eventually, the 15 minutes grew into 30 minutes and then even longer.

I made sure to put aside this time strictly for God. I made it a priority to have no interruptions. No social media, phone, TV, or browsing the Internet. This was God's time. The more I spent time in His Word, the more I saw a change in my heart. And, the more I saw a change in my heart, the more I saw a transformation in my character. The more He perfected my character, the more my life was fashioned in the greatness He designed for me to be.

As a result, eventually, I was healed. Eventually, I felt free. Ladies, freedom is a beautiful thing. You don't have to stay in bondage! No man has a say over your freedom! I urge every woman to remove the *cover girl* mask from your face. It's time to stop pretending and it's time to be real with yourself. It's time to take your life and your identity into your hands and stop willingly putting it in the hands of the counterfeit. You are a beautiful creature designed for a perfect mate. Until the time comes for God to introduce you to your purpose partner, let God be your foundation. Let Him build you into that God-fearing woman. You are a queen and queens do not subject themselves to jokers. Remember, you are God's girl. And anything that is connected to God, is connected to greatness.

PRAY ON PURPOSE

I am not a *cover girl*, but I am covered in Christ. God, I thank you for rescuing my heart from the darkness. Thank you for bringing me back to your marvelous light. God, continue to be the source of my life. God, continue to be the strength of my life. God, continue to allow your Word to search my heart and my soul. God, I want your Word to be the all-consuming fire in my life. If you find anything that shouldn't be, I want you to burn it out my life. Let your Word refine me, Oh Lord! Let your Word renew me, Oh Lord! Let your Word restore me, Oh Lord! In Jesus' name, Amen.

3

FINDING YOUR POWER

"For God has not given us a spirit of fear, but of power and of love and of a sound mind." II Timothy 1:7 NKJV

"Get up!" My mother said as she pulled back the curtains and slowly raised the blinds. The afternoon light greeted my face. Not interested in its sweet hello, I pulled the covers up over my head. "Get up," she implored me a second time. I heard her, but I didn't move. Trying to avoid my mother and her intuition, I made up a lousy excuse for staying in bed. "Please mom, I'm tired. I just want to sleep."

But, my mother wasn't having it. She walked over beside my bed and pulled off every cover, exposing me from head to toe. "You cannot hide anymore, baby. You cannot stay in bed forever. Eventually, you'll have to get up. As long as I am still living, I will not allow you to sleep your life away. It's time to get up for Brittany. It's time to get up for the people who will need to hear your story."

You never know how powerful you are, until you are faced with a situation that requires you to call on the depths of your inner resources, just to put one foot in front of the other. Can I be real with you? I had been in bed for two days. I did not want to eat. I did not want to talk. I did not want to leave the room. I was heartbroken.

Here's the tea.

THE PRETENDER

Have you ever met someone and thought, "this person could be the one?" Well, this guy had every item on the *what I want in a guy checklist*. Yes, I had a checklist. He was intelligent, dark, tall, charming, driven, and successful. Our dates were full of laughter and spontaneity. From lunch dates in the city to horseback riding in the country, he was a complete gentleman. We had been courting for three months and everything seemed to be going well, until he told me, "I can't see you anymore."

Just like that, out of the blue, he said that he couldn't date me anymore because he didn't believe what I believed. When we first started dating, I told him that I was active in my church and that I valued my relationship with God. I also told him that I was waiting until marriage.

At first, he seemed okay with this. But as time progressed, and time will always eventually reveal all truth, Mr. Pretender could not pretend any longer. Was I heartbroken? Yes, I was. I had shared so much of myself, and invited him into my life and circle of friends. I even introduced him to my parents. Still, I was heartbroken when he dropped me. For once in my life, I felt like I had met the right guy. I thought he had everything I ever wanted and more.

A few days after we parted ways, I received a phone call from my friend Jay. He asked me if I was still talking to the guy in D.C. I told him, "No, he called it off with me." "Good," he said. When I asked Jay why he would say something like that, he explained that my "Mr. Prince Charming" was not so charming. Come to find out, not only was he talking to me, but he was also in a relationship with another woman on the side. I was in shock. Like most women do, I checked my resources and learned that what Jay said was actually true.

After hearing the news that Mr. Pretender had been dating someone else, it was like someone *flipped a switch*. I immediately went from hope to hurt, from joy to depression, from freedom to fear. I started telling myself that this was my fate, that *I will never experience true love*. I don't know about you, but when I love, I love hard. And when the one I commit to hurts me, I hurt even harder. I gave so much of my power to the breakup, that I neglected to see God's blessing in the "level up."

THE ABUSER

Many of us operate in fear, before and after a breakup. I can recall one relationship where I sacrificed my own needs for the sake of keeping the relationship. I like to refer to him as Mr. Abuser. He was charming on the outside, toned physique, tall, dark, and a smooth talker. He knew how to say the right things at the right time. However, behind closed doors he was a manipulator. He knew how to play on my emotions when he wanted to use me for my money. However, when he couldn't get what he wanted, he would verbally and emotionally abuse me. He would tear down my self-esteem by calling me useless, worthless, and stupid. My friends would constantly ask, "Why are you putting yourself through this? Is he really worth it?" I would cover up by saying, "It's not like that...he's not like that...we're not like that." But deep down inside, I wanted them to rescue me from the brokenness I felt.

When you give someone control over you they can break you mentally and physically. I was ashamed to tell my loved ones that I was mentally and physically powerless with this person. I felt powerless to think for myself. Powerless to speak for myself. Powerless to move for myself. Fear played a huge part on why I could not function as the queen God created me to be. I was so broken in the relationship that his abusive influence swayed me to believe that I would never love again. So, I remained silent and stagnate to keep him.

I stayed because after he would belittle me, he would apologize and tell me, "I love you baby. I can't control myself. My past makes me act this way." His words would manipulate my heart in such a way that I trusted him. He would often share with me about his broken childhood and how he watched his father abused his mother. And my compassion led me to think that if I left him now, I would be added to the list of those who neglected him. Even though the verbal abuse became worse, I stayed because I wanted to prove to him that I wasn't like his father. I wanted to be that nurturer he never had. I wanted him to know that I was everything he needed. Even though he couldn't provide me with what I needed.

RELEASING FEAR

I continued to operate in fear after the breakup. Although I left the abusive relationship, I didn't leave the fear. Fear persuaded me to believe that I was nothing without him. That I would never be able to move on with my life or walk in my purpose. Fear persuaded me to believe that all men were dogs and that all women were gold diggers (at least the ones that were after my man). Not only did I allow fear to move into my heart, but I also welcomed its cousins: distrust, anxiety, and self-doubt. I was so bogged down with these roommates that I couldn't find the strength to evict them from my heart.

One night as I was journaling, I was reflecting on the next phase of my life. I asked myself the question, "What would my life look like without fear?" For so long, I was afraid of my abusive ex, afraid of moving forward, and afraid of being hurt again. Tears began to flow down my cheeks. As I wrote my thoughts, it was clear my soul yearned for freedom, and it directed me to make a decision for my purpose. That's when

God told me that I had to release the power of fear. When we don't release fear it becomes a heavyweight. It leads you in the wrong direction, and makes you believe that you are not worth it. It was imperative for me to take matters into my own hands and refuse to allow fear to lead me away from my destiny.

The first step I took, was to denounce the spirit of fear over my life, my heart, my mind, and my purpose. I declared that *whatever happened before the breakup would never happen again*. I declared that *whatever happened after the breakup would never follow me into my future*. Know this...you have the power over your today and your tomorrow. You have the power to rise up. You have the power to speak up. You have the power to stand. You are resilient! No one should ever have control over your heart, mind, soul, and destiny.

Secondly, I chose to start following a positive diet plan. This consisted of feeding myself only positive thoughts and starving myself of negative ones. When you subject yourself to fear, it drains your energy, increases your insecurities, and steals your power. When you nourish your heart and mind with faith, peace, and goodness, your purpose is able to flourish. Your purpose cannot grow in a fearful mindset. As long as you remain in a negative mindset, your purpose will remain unclear and stagnant.

Ladies and gents, when it came to finding my purpose, I had to make a conscious decision to no longer settle in fear. I had to make a conscious decision that no man would ever take my power again. I embraced the anthem: *Yes, I am brand new*. I was *determined to find* my power. I was *determined to build* my power. I was *determined to work* my power. I was *determined to protect* my power.

Once you make the decision to own your power, your past will always try to find a way to stop you. Don't you find it funny that as soon as you decide to move on with your life, that a text or an email will suddenly pop up from your ex? You will get the *I miss you, I love you, I need you, you are my heart, I realized I cannot do life without you* messages. The moment you take steps to move forward, you can almost always expect one.

Why is that? Why does your past find ways to interrupt your healing journey? It's simple. When that ex recognizes that you are operating in the power of your purpose, they will do anything to disrupt it. Not only do they see the power that is growing inside of you, but they do not want it to exist. Why? Because they are intimidated. They recognize that once you hone your power, you hone your destiny. While you were with them, you couldn't see your purpose or the blessings that God had for you. That broken relationship had a stronghold over your heart, mind, body, and soul. But when you got out of that broken relationship, you woke up. Once you grabbed hold of your power, you started positioning yourself to move into new territories. You started recognizing that God was opening doors for your purpose. You were no longer being held captive for what they wanted you to be. You realized you have your own power. You found your voice and started maximizing the power that God gave you.

So, let's recap! If I could repeat anything from this chapter, I would say, "Never give your power away to any man or woman." When you give someone your power, you become a puppet to them. When you give your power away, you become incompetent, insufficient, and inadequate. Scripture says, "we are more than a conqueror through him that loved us" (Romans 8:37 KJV). If you are in this place now, I urge you to cut every string that has ever been attached to you. I want you to denounce the fear, the self-doubt, and the anxiety. I want you to denounce every verbal and mental abuse that anyone has spoken over you. When God created you, He made greatness. He made a conqueror. Every lie that has been spoken over you is now under your feet. Repeat after me: *I am sufficient! I am adequate! I am in control of my destiny! I've got the power!*

PRAY ON PURPOSE

Today, I take back my power. I take back the keys to my purpose. No longer will I place my purpose in the hands of someone that does not love me. No longer will I submit to negative thinking, negative people, and negative relationships. I am a daughter/son of a King; therefore, I deserve more. I deserve to be happy. I deserve peace. I deserve the best. God, I pray that you will give me the tools to build my power. I also pray that you continue to give me the strength to work my power. In Jesus' name, Amen.

4

FINDING YOUR STRENGTH

"But those who trust in the Lord will find new strength. They will soar high on wings like eagles. They will run and not grow weary. They will walk and not faint." Isaiah 40:31 NLT

I've never been a fan of running. But somehow, I was starting to feel like my mind was running a marathon. I would think things like:

"How could he do this?"

"How could she do this?"

"Will I ever find the strength to move on?"

I was replaying thoughts of the betrayal, thoughts of the lies, and thoughts of the other women. My mind was in a constant battle with itself. No matter how hard I tried to let them go, the thoughts continued to torment me. I felt insecure to a level I never imagined possible. I felt in a constant state of unworthiness.

If you've ever been cheated on, I dedicate this chapter to you. I know what it's like to feel that you're not beautiful enough, not smart enough, not interesting enough...simply not enough. I know what it's like to feel embarrassed and undeserving at the same time. I know what it's like to value commitment and loyalty to its fullest, but yet, it means nothing to your significant other. I know what it's like to feel you've wasted so much time and that you'll never get it back. Yes, I know what it feels like to be in the same room with the man you know you love and the woman you know he is cheating with. I know what it feels like to be an option and not a priority, and to go places as a couple and see his eyes on someone else. *I know what it feels like.*

THE WARNING SEASON

Cheating in a relationship is a selfish, dishonest action. It obstructs the trust and taints the love that you've worked to build over time. God began to speak to me in my dreams each night about my then boyfriend. Most people would call it a sign, I referred to it as my *Warning Season*. God was constantly trying to reveal to me the things he was doing behind my back.

In my dreams I saw my boyfriend flirting and having sex with his exes. I would confront him and each time he would deny it, dismissing me saying, "You're delusional. What are you talking about? I'm not messing with anyone." My heart wanted to believe him, but my instincts screamed, "Girl, wake up! He's lying!" Word of advice. Never discredit your instincts. You are not delusional. You are not crazy. If something inside of you screams *something is off* about a person, trust it.

As I will mention throughout this book, I stayed with him because I felt like things could work out. I was raised to believe in forgiveness. The Bible says, "Lord, how often will my brother sin against me, and I forgive him? As many as seven times?" Jesus said to him, "I do not say to you seven times, but seventy-seven times" (Matthew 18:21-22 ESV). I naively believed that he deserved a second, third, and even a tenth chance.

One evening, as I pulled into the driveway after driving home from work, a Facebook notification popped up on my phone. I parked my car, opened the message, and there it was right before my eyes. To this day, it still baffles me how God orchestrated this exposure. Let me emphasize, I didn't have access to his profile. I have no idea how or why the messages for his account started appearing on my phone.

As I scrolled through the message, tears began to roll down my face. Each comment was like a knife in my heart. One said, "You've been on my mind like crazy...I miss you...If things don't work out with my current girlfriend, I'm giving us one more chance." My heart felt like it sank to the floor. I felt angry and sad at the same time.

How could he play on both of our emotions like this? How could he say that he loved me? This whole time, he convinced me that the dreams God was sending me were my imagination, that I had conjured them up in my head. This was not the first nor the last time this happened. The messages never stopped, and he continued to sleep with his exes. He repeatedly apologized and convinced me it would never happen again. And each time I would take him back. Why, you ask? I truly believed if I left him, I was giving up on the relationship, quitting on the future we could possibly have.

I have a philosophy about cheating that many people find interesting. I think staying with the cheater is equally as bad as the cheating itself. I know some of you won't be happy with that statement, but hear me out. I can hear people saying, "What about counseling for married couples who want to stay together? People can change, so how can you make that statement?"

I can only speak from my experiences as a single woman. I cannot speak for married couples because I've never been married. Do I think people can change? Absolutely, there's no doubt in my mind. But I do know this, they have to change for themselves. You cannot force them to change.

Truth be told, I damaged myself more by staying than I would've been had I walked away. How? Because, as often as he would tell me he would never do it again, he always went back to messing around. Yes, he convinced me that we would go through counseling. Yes, he promised me, on bended knee, that I was the only one that he loved and the "others" did not matter. But on the other side, when I chose to stay, everything that was promised to my heart eventually fell to the ground. When I stayed, the cheating and the lies continued.

I stayed, and the arguments tripled, and the tears flowed like rivers. I spent countless sleepless nights wondering if he was at home or out with another woman. I tormented myself mentally and emotionally, and the effects showed outwardly.

There were times where I knew I had to get up at 3:00am for work. I'd be on the phone with him until all hours of the night, arguing about one of his "women." Suddenly, I'd realize it was 12 am or 1 am and I'd only have two or three hours to sleep.

My friends kept asking me, "Why do you put yourself through all of this? You are much too beautiful to suffer this way." But, I chose to stay in this place of torment because I loved him, so I thought. I wanted to prove that I was his "ride or die" chick.

I stayed, because I did not want to let go of my two-year investment. Truth be told, I was slowly dying on the inside. I convinced myself that he would change for the better like he promised. I hoped eventually he would get the need to have multiple women out of his system. I tried to assure myself that he really loved me.

On the verge of leaving the relationship, I had to come to terms with myself. I wanted God to show me what I was missing. But what He showed me was, that by staying, I was dishonoring my own worth. God showed me that as long as I stayed, I was cheating on my own purpose. I was pouring so much of my love into a dead relationship, when I should have been pouring love into God, myself, and my purpose.

BUBBLES AND BROKENNESS

I ran myself a hot bubble bath. The hot steam rose up around my body as tears rolled down my cheeks. Have you ever been so disgusted with your decisions that you want it to wash all the way? I'd often take a bubble bath just to try and wash away the hurt and abuse I felt from him. I sat in there for a long time, that my hands and feet were pruned. And, finally came to the realization that I had neglected my purpose in order to have the title of girlfriend. In that moment, God showed me how selfish I had been toward His will for my life. A heart to heart with God does not always yield flowers and rainbows, sometimes His message is hard to swallow, but His discipline is worth it.

I've made many mistakes in my life when it comes to relationships. But, through all of my bad choices, God has always had mercy on me. As scripture says, "He brought me up also out of a horrible pit, out of the miry clay, and set my feet upon a rock, and established my goings" (Psalm 40:2 KJV). It took God's strength to carry me out of that abusive relationship. It took His strength to transform me into the person I am today: confident, happy, and powerful.

STRENGTH TRAINING

When I finally opened my heart to God, He became my strength trainer. If you workout at all, you know, strength training can do a number of great things for you. It increases your endurance, helps you lose weight, builds your muscles, and improves your core. If we apply that concept in a spiritual sense, we will see that God does the same thing for our lives. When God takes you through spiritual strength training, He is "perfecting you, establishing you, strengthening you, and settling you" (1 Peter 5:10 KJV). In this training, God teaches you how to find your own strength, build your spirit, and improve your spiritual core. When it comes to relationships, God is teaching you that the best kind of weight you can lose is that of an unhealthy one. Unhealthy relationships are not worth losing sleep over, losing yourself, or losing your purpose.

I encourage those who find yourself struggling to leave an unhealthy relationship or unpromising situationship, to get out quickly! Your purpose depends on it. God has a greater purpose for you, and you cannot waste your time with a counterfeit person or relationship. I pray you find the strength to leave and never look back like I did.

When I finally chose to walk away from this particular guy, I felt so free on the inside. It was more than a weight that had been lifted off my shoulders, it felt like I was shedding off pounds of dead skin. For so long, I wore the weight of my past. It kept my heart dark and my mind clogged with bitterness, guilt, and hurt. It was when my word lined up with my deed, that everything in my life began to change for the better. I wasn't worried about who the next man would be. All I wanted was God. All I desired was for God to take me into his loving arms and to restore me anew.

When I announced to my ex that I was done, I said it with authority. I let him know that there was nothing he could say or do that would change my mind. I was done trying to figure out whether he loved me or not. I was done trying to figure out whether he was still messing with his ex or not. I was done with his lies and secrets. I was done with his verbal abuse. I was done with the insecurities. Instead of choosing pain, my heart chose forgiveness. I *forgave myself* and *forgave him* for everything he had done. I wholeheartedly wished him all the best. I told him to *move on* with his life and that *we were better off separate than together*. It was the best, long awaited decision I've ever made. If I had to change anything, it would be that I would have ended the relationship sooner.

If you find yourself in a similar, or any difficult situation, I pray that you open your heart to God and give him free reign over your life. It's time to get out of that dark place, put on your strength gear, and start you're training. There's a purpose that you are training for. You have to be strong to carry your purpose into your destiny. There's no time for distractions. The training may be intense, but it is preparing you for the destiny that God has for you.

PRAY ON PURPOSE

Dear God, give me the strength to move past my hurts. Give me the courage to exit this place of torment and enter into a place of peace. Forgive me for cheating on my purpose and being selfish to your will. I am ready to start spiritual strength training. I am ready for you to teach me how to build my spiritual core. God, I want you to take off any weight that will hinder me from reaching your will. Please remove me from every relationship that will cause damage to my purpose. In Jesus' name, Amen.

5

FINDING THE WILL

"I'm not saying that I have this all together, that I have it made.
But I am well on my way, reaching out for Christ, who has so
wondrously reached out for me. Friends, don't get me wrong:
By no means do I count myself an expert in all of this, but I've
got my eye on the goal, where God is beckoning us onward - to
Jesus. I'm off and running, and I'm not turning back."
Philippians 3:12-14 MSG

Everyone has a favorite pair of jeans. Regardless if your
hips are wider, thighs are thicker, or your love handles are
talking, you are determined to wear them as often as you can.
In fact, you have mastered the "squeeze." You don't care how
ridiculous you may look: jumping around, double dipping,
counseling yourself in the mirror, and holding your breath.
You have conditioned yourself to believe that this behavior is
normal.

You may have other options to choose from, but you prefer to wear this pair. Why? They make your body feel magical. Sometimes these jeans have holes in places that shouldn't be…but we tell ourselves, "That's okay, ripped jeans are the trend." These jeans can be so tight that we cannot breathe and air cannot circulate between the fabric and our skin. "But that's okay," we tell ourselves, "tight jeans are the trend." We have perfected the "but that's okay" excuse. And, this brings me to several questions. Is the style the trend? Or, is your complacency the trend? Has your comfort ever made you look uncomfortable?

Sadly, that's how we are. We hold on to things of the past, like jeans that no longer fit or look good on us, and we refuse to let go. We can have so many holes in our relationship: dishonesty, abuse, cheating, etc., that there is no room for workable space and no signs of fresh air.

All the warning signs indicate that the relationship is toxic. We can see that the relationship is not working out. We can see that our personalities don't mesh. We can see that the love is not there. We can have all the signs of cheating. We know we have outgrown each other, but we stay anyway, even in an unhealthy environment. We choose to remain in the habit of pain that makes us feel that we do not deserve better, and that it's okay to be stuck.

SPRING CLEANING

Why do we refuse to let go of the person God has commanded us to let go of? Easy, we are creatures of complacency. The longer you stay, the more addicted you become. We label addictions to drugs and alcohol, but do you know people can be addictions too? There are people we like to hold on to. These people have helped to fill certain voids. Like all addictions, these people are only meant to give you a temporary fix. They make you feel good and look good, only for a moment.

In a ten year span, I was addicted to dating a B.O.B, a "boy of baggage." Because I didn't love myself or value who I was, I allowed B.O.B to have full control of my heart and my mind. To the point where B.O.B manipulated my heart and my mind. As long as I was with him, I didn't care how he treated me. Although it hurt me to my core, I was a forgiving person and always believed that B.O.B would change one day. Well, one day was never. Deep down inside, I knew that my parents didn't raise me to be treated that way, and even deeper, I knew God did not create me to be in a worthless relationship.

Letting go can be one of the hardest things to do. Why? Because no one likes to be uncomfortable. Why hold on to people, especially when they don't fit in God's will? Why continue to hold on to people who are filled with emptiness? We become junkies, torn between our pain and the greatness God has for us.

When I was a teenager, I remember wanting to spring clean my room. It was my junior year in high school and I wanted to make some changes to my wardrobe. I was about to enter college, a new chapter in my life. I wanted to make space in my closet for all the new things I would be getting for college.

I stood in the middle of the closet just staring at all of the stuff. There was so much of it, shirts, sweaters, dresses, skirts, bags, shoes, and sandals. So much stuff that it would take me days to finish. I had clothes and shoes dating back to middle school. What in the world was I doing with this old stuff? There was no question that I had outgrown it. I realized that I needed to let go.

Spring cleaning is sometimes necessary in our lives too. It opens your eyes to baggage that you thought you got rid of. Spiritually, that's how God feels about us. A spiritual cleanse is necessary in order to find your purpose. If you have so much clutter in your life and continue to hold on to your past, you will never possess the freedom that God has ordained in your life.

If you are seeking to find your purpose, it's time to let the baggage go. It's time to get rid of old people, old ways, old habits, old traditions, and old lifestyles. There's no time to waste when your destiny awaits. Greater is ahead of you. Greater is awaiting your arrival. It is time to let go of the hurt, pain, sin, defeats, frustrations, the mistakes, the past, the rejection, and the lies.

Trust me when I say, *letting go always benefits your purpose.* Because when you let go, there is something always better waiting for you. Learn from the mistakes I made, holding on to outdated things and toxic people, will delay your arrival to your destiny. I made so many excuses for why I should stay. I mastered the "squeeze." Constantly talking myself into fitting into a relationship that was not designed for me. I held my breath so many times to try and save a toxic relationship. Honey, trust me when I say, it's not worth it.

God is calling you to pursue your vision. It's long overdue. You are supposed to publish that book, record that song, start that business, apply for that job, finish that degree, audition for that role. I know you hear God's voice telling you to leave that relationship. Don't ignore it, trust God's voice. Trust the instincts He has placed on the inside. Move to the rhythm of God's voice. Everything has a time and season. Don't miss out on your season of destiny. Don't miss out on the wardrobe change God has for you. You cannot wear old clothes in new seasons. God will move greatly on your behalf, when you choose to break from the bondage, and step out into the purpose He has designed for you.

PRAY ON PURPOSE

Dear God, show me the things that I am holding on to. Purge me from every addiction. I want to be free from every toxic relationship. I want to be free from the lies, guilt, shame, and anger. Give me the power to "Let It Go." I don't want anything to hinder me from reaching my blessings. You have so much prepared for me. I realize my destiny awaits me. Open my ears to hear your voice. I submit my will to yours. There is a new season that you want me to walk into. Let me tap into this new season. Prepare and equip me to be ready for this season. In Jesus' name, Amen.

Part II

What does **L.O.V.E.** mean?

In this section, we will learn how to "**Let Our Values Echo**." So many of us have never learned or have lost this very important value of loving ourselves. When you learn to love yourself, you will refuse to settle for anything less than what you know God has in store for you. The love you display within, will echo to others on how to love and value you. When you love yourself, not only do you learn to set standards and boundaries, but you learn to commit to them.

6

THE POTTER AND THE CLAY

"Who in the world do you think you are to second-guess God?
Do you for one moment suppose any of us knows enough to
call God into question? Clay doesn't talk back to the fingers that
mold it, saying, "Why did you shape me like this?" Isn't it
obvious that a potter has a perfect right to shape one lump of
clay into a vase for holding flowers and another into a pot for
cooking beans?" Romans 9:20-21 MSG

I traded long bus rides home for after school programs to
avoid the bullies. I can remember hurrying down the long
hallways of elementary school hoping and praying to get to my
classroom without being noticed. I recall their shadows, their
laughs, and the grenades they carried in their mouths:

"Oink, Oink! Ms. Piggy!"

"U-G-L-Y!"

"Rash Girl!"

I was eight years old when my family moved to Virginia. And, I was also eight years old when the bullying began. My father was in the Army stationed overseas in Korea. My mother was working two jobs. During the day, she was a full-time sales manager at a Fortune 500 company, and at night she worked part-time at Costco to make ends meet.

My parents were hard workers and always wanted the best for their children. They sacrificed a lot just to give us the very best, even if it required taking on another job. While my mother was at work, my grandparents took care of my brothers and I. I didn't know how to tell my parents about the fear, sadness, and pain I felt at school every day. How does an eight year old tell her family that there are monsters, not underneath her bed, but in the hallways of her school, in her classrooms, and in her mind?

I didn't understand why God had created me as He had, or why my parents made us move to Virginia. I had such fond memories of our life in Texas, the warm sunshine, the delicious foods and cuisines, my unbiased friends, and the freedom I felt to be myself and to live jubilantly.

Moving to Virginia was the opposite of that. I would hide behind my grandfather's chair in the living room. It was the one place I could escape the teasing I experienced outside the walls of the place I now called "home." I believe that's where the root of my constant feelings of being rejected began.

The truth is, I hated everything about myself. I hated my nose, my height, and the eczema that covered my body from

45

head to toe. I despised the daily oatmeal baths my doctor recommended and the stench of skin ointments and creams. Winter was my friend, I could cover up the eczema with sweaters and long pants. But, summer was my enemy. I'd wear long sleeves in the summer, just to hide the rashes on my arms. It could be 100 degrees outside, but you could still find me wearing my favorite blue corduroy pants and a turtleneck shirt.

The teasing lasted throughout middle school. Kids would tease me the most about my nose. They would spread their noses to make it look like a pig. My nose was flat and wide, and because it was not pointed like there's, my nickname around school was "Miss Piggy." I would often run inside the girl's bathroom stall, but I would never cry in front of them. I was afraid it would just incite them to say worse, even meaner things.

I would lie in bed at night and cry out to God. I would literally question my own existence. "Why couldn't You make me a normal child? Why couldn't You give me normal skin and a normal nose? Why didn't You make me beautiful? Why did You create me, God? What is my purpose here on this earth?"

At 11, I started creating lists titled: *What I do not like about Brittany and What they did not like about me.* I would write things like: "You'll never be anything, you're so ugly, you'll never be loved and you're so stupid." I allowed these negative opinions about myself and my feelings of rejection and insecurity to rule my life. The lists became my manifestos. Not only were the bullies against me, but I bullied myself and my purpose.

COUNTERFEITS

The things I said and thought about myself damaged me. And, as I grew older, I became what I believed. I did not love myself inwardly, and it was obvious on the outside. My lack of self-esteem became particularly evident in my choice of men. I was broken and insecure and that's the kind of men I attracted. If a man called me beautiful, I accepted all of his flaws, no matter how bad they were, because those words soothed the insecurities I had about how I looked.

Have you ever dated someone that said all the right things, but their actions said something different? I dated all kinds of established men, professional athletes to businessmen, and they all followed the same trend: they were what I like to call "counterfeits." A counterfeit is a knockoff imitation of the real deal. They closely resemble your purpose partner, however; they are not the mate that God has chosen for you.

Every time I broke up with a counterfeit, I would vow never to fall for one again. But, I always did. My mother would warn me, "He is no good Brittany!" But, I didn't listen. I would promise her I had everything under control and that I wouldn't let anything distract me from my purpose. But, I would continuously find myself in counterfeit traps.

There was a guy I dated in college. He had an athletic built, he was mocha brown and tall...the way I liked them. It's amazing how the devil will play on what you like. He will send you people that have a fine appearance, but they are far from

47

being fine for you. On the outside he looked good, but on the inside his character was totally opposite. My mother warned me, "Brittany, stay away from that guy. He's not the one for you. He's going to hurt you in the end. He's only after one thing." Did I listen? Absolutely not. I told her, "It's not like that. We're just cool, Mom." *We're just cool*, turn into me being a complete fool. Everything my mother said was true. He lied about seeing other women, he lied about having a baby, he lied about loving me. He pretty much lied about everything.

BUILDING MY CONFIDENCE

My mother continued to pray, and I guess God had finally had enough of my disobedience too, because one day His grace spoke to me.

I was sitting in my dorm room by myself. My roommate had gone home for the weekend. My friends had invited me to a party, but I didn't want to go because I knew my ex would be there. I was literally over everything and everyone. It was a Friday night and I had my room all to myself, so I decided to stay in. I wanted to watch a movie and just relax. I went to the drawer where I kept the DVDs to find something to watch and came across an inspirational young adult book that I had forgotten that I had. It was a high school graduation gift.

I opened it up and the word *purpose* seemed to jump off the page. I believe in that moment, God drew me to that word. He was sending me a message. He wanted me to see that I didn't have to live my life outside of the purpose he had for me. In that moment, I heard God say, "I created you Brittany for My greater purpose. You have been chosen by me to fulfill My will. You have been chosen by Me to speak life to others. You have been chosen by Me to lead a movement."

This was huge, and I knew it. I stood there with the book in my hand, staring at the page. I had been chosen by God. I was "a royal priesthood, a holy nation, God's special possession" (1 Peter 2:9 NIV). In that moment, I knew my main purpose on this earth is to heal others. I was to impact the lost and help lead them to their destinies.

None of us were set on this earth to just exist and then wilt away. Like me, you too were created, "to not die, but live, and declare the works of the Lord" (Psalm 118:17 KJV). If you've ever questioned your existence, your smarts, your looks, and carried the weight of those insecurities with you, now is the time to free yourself.

There is nothing wrong with the way you look. There is nothing wrong with the shape of your body or your weight or your size. There is nothing wrong with your skin type or your color. We are all shaped in God's image. Which means we are shaped by His perfect love and beauty. God made you exactly how He wanted you to be. There is only one you. I encourage you to learn to embrace your uniqueness in every way. The world is tired of the trends, it is waiting to see you live out your authenticity.

I had to get to a place in myself where I would never allow anyone to make me feel like I lacked in "good looks." I was determined to never fall for any guy just to soothe my insecurities. There was a point in my life that I wanted to have plastic surgery on my nose and breast because I did not like how they were shaped. I felt if I had a smaller nose and a bigger cup size that it would make me a beautiful woman.

One day, I came across an older lady as I was walking to my car. She said, "Hey beautiful! God made you just the way you are. Embrace it." I don't know who she was or where she came from, but I knew my heart was supposed to hear what she had to say. And, she was right. God made me this way. And when God creates, he makes no mistakes. I realize that I was more than a conqueror through Christ (Romans 8:37 KJV). I allowed that scripture to be my motivation for my life.

So you ask, how did I build my confidence? To build my self-esteem, I started with my mind. Every day I would repeat daily affirmations like: *I am beautiful. I am worth the wait. I am wonderfully made. I am a queen.*

In addition to building my confidence, I started working out. The more I worked out, the more confident I became with my body. I started to feel healthier and stronger in my emotions, mind, and physique. The more steps I took toward my well-being, the more my confidence grew. To maintain this level of confidence, I sought God for wisdom. Scripture says, "if any of you lacks wisdom, let him ask of God, who gives to all liberally and without reproach, and it will be given to him"

(James 1:5 NKJV). It was amazing how God was giving me wisdom on how to pursue a well-rounded life.

He showed me how important it was to take care of my temple (1 Corinthians 6:19 KJV). In fact, the scripture speaks of how "physical exercise and spiritual exercise have value" (1 Timothy 4:8 GNT). I encourage you to explore and try new things that will help build your confidence; whether it be exercising, participating in a recreational activity or quoting daily inspirational affirmations. It's never too late to build your confidence.

You may ask, why is it important to be confident? How do purpose and confidence coincide? It is important that you have a strong confidence because where you are going requires a grounded person. Your destiny cannot be obtained fully if you're not confident in yourself and the path that God is taking you on. God had to build my confidence because he knew what my purpose consisted of. He knew that I would be an author, a purpose coach, and a businesswoman.

God knows your purpose too and He wants you to take charge of your destiny. In order for me to take charge of my purpose, God had to get me to a level where I was mentally, emotionally, spiritually, and physically healthy. Not only do you have to know where you are going, but you must believe in where you are going.

My mother would always tell me, "Brittany you cannot be weak minded when it comes to what God has for you. You have to walk confidently, believe confidently, and talk confidently."

My goal in this book is to help you to be all God has created you to be. To uplift your confidence and stir up the gift inside of you. You have amazing gifts that are awaiting to be activated. Remember, time waits for no one. Let today be your day to pursue your purpose fearlessly.

PRAY ON PURPOSE

Forgive me for questioning the Potter. I cast down every insecurity and negative thought about myself. I command every vain imagination to be uprooted out of my life. My God did not create me out of sadness, but He created me in joy. I will live in this joy, that I am wonderfully made. I will live in this joy, that I will embrace my uniqueness. I will live in this joy, that I do not have to subject myself to people's opinions. I will live in this joy, that I will not allow anyone to soothe my insecurities. I will live in this joy, that I will not fall for counterfeits or their traps.

God, I recognize you shaped me into the person you created me to be. Lord, I embrace that there is one me and I will live my authenticity out loud. Build my confidence, Lord! Activate my gifts, Lord! Push me God to be all that I need to be for my purpose and destiny. In Jesus' name, Amen.

7

CONFESSIONS FROM THE BAYOU

"If we confess our sins, He is faithful and just to forgive us our sins, and to cleanse us from all unrighteousness."
1 John 1:9 NKJV

Tessa wanted to talk with me alone, but when I suggested we meet at a cafe downtown she said, "No. I don't want anyone to see me like this." "Where would you like to meet?" I asked. "I'd rather we meet at my car," she explained. "I'm parked in the back parking lot of Walmart." I gathered my things and told her I was on the way.

I arrived and saw her grey Honda Accord parked in a dark corner, her headlights turned off. As I approached the car, I could see through the driver's seat window the fear of condemnation and shame rimming Tessa's sweet mocha brown eyes. I opened the door and slid into the front passenger seat. I had barely closed the door when Tessa cried out, "My parents will never forgive me!"

Tessa was just like me, a good ole' church girl. We both loved and valued our relationship with God. Our respective upbringings were indistinguishable, including our parents, who were ministers in the church. I rested my hand on Tessa's shoulder and assured her it would be okay. Her tears spoke of her disappointment in herself, her family, and her God. She spoke as if she was flawed and had been defiled and exploited.

I could identify with Tessa's story all too well. I cried along with her as she confessed that she was no longer a virgin. She stared into my eyes looking for a response. The only words I could manage to say were, "We will get through this together." Little did she know, for years, I wore the same mask, struggled with the same secret. Now, as I look back on that moment, I question my bravery. *Why didn't I open up to Tessa? Why didn't I share the truth that I was not a virgin either?*

I was raised to never open up about your past because people will judge you and use it against you. I remained obedient to those instructions and held my tongue for the sake of not embarrassing my family's or the church's reputation. These "legalisms" were created to keep my testimony silent and were causing me more pain than healing. The longer I held onto my secret, the more I felt my integrity corroding from the inside out.

Church events were the hardest days for me. I would hear preachers speak on the evils of fornication, praising how they kept their virginity, and condemning those who have not. Let me pause right here. No, I am not opposed to sexual purity. No, I am not opposed to keeping your virginity. No, I am not opposed to being obedient to the Word of God. I believe, we all should strive for sexual purity and to wait on our purpose mate, as God intended in His Word. I believe, we all should wait until marriage to have sex. I believe, we all should obey His Word and abstain from sexual immorality. However, I do not believe in condemning someone who is not a virgin and making them feel less than who they are. In my eyes, they are still a child of God. In my eyes, God can redeem them to be a born again virgin.

As I would look around the congregation, I would see the look of shame and discomfort wash over the "non-virgin" faces, including mine. When they were called out to come forward to the altar to be delivered from their lustful sins, I would see the "church folk" whispering judgements with their eyes. I was afraid to be judged, so I remained in my seat, hands folded, mouth shut, eyes forward. Sometimes I wanted to run up to every person at the altar and shout, "I understand your struggle! You are not alone!" I wanted to tell people that it was going to be okay, and that they were forgiven. However, the "reputation" of *others* kept me bound and in my seat.

I often wondered if "church folk" could see my skeletons? Could they tell I was not the "saint" they thought I was? I battled with these thoughts for 12 years. I sought an escape, because I was tired of being chained. I was ready to be free. I was ready to be open about who I was and what I had become for the better.

CONFESSION NO. 2

Before college, the only thing I knew was church, school, and my after school job. I was oblivious about anything outside of those things. My parents raised me in a sheltered, Christian environment. So that meant, I never went to parties, I never drank alcohol, I never smoked, and I never had sex. Like any loving parents, my mother and father raised me the best way they knew how. Till this day, much of my success and my focused-driven character I can attribute to my upbringing. And, I truly thank my parents for that.

Looking back, I understand that my parents wanted to raise their children on Godly principles and to keep us from the mistakes they made in the past. Therefore, church was my life and my life was the church. We were the first ones there and the last ones to leave. We were at every conference, every revival, every Bible study, every Sunday service, every youth service, every prayer service...basically every church function. Unlike most kids, I didn't mind going to church because I always had a love for God. I had a strong hunger and thirst for a relationship with God. To the point where I accepted Christ at the age of 10 and was filled with the Holy Spirit. I was determined that nothing could separate me from the love of God. For 17 years, I held onto the Christian standards and values I was taught. That is, until I went the college.

CONFESSION NO. 3

When I arrived on my college campus, I felt something I had never felt before...independence. And with it, many of the things my parents told me not to do went straight out the window. For the first time in my life, I had no curfew. I could go out and do as I please. And I did.

I had never been to a club or to a house party, so I was ready to experience all the fun (insert twerk here). College social life was enticing and exciting to me. Every weekend, I partied, met new friends, and lived a chaperone-free life. At one particular house party, I met a guy. He was tall, mocha brown, and handsome, with an athletic build, just the way I like them.

We caught each other's attention and we exchanged phone numbers. He seemed like a pretty nice guy. Weeks later, we started dating and things became very serious, fast. I can remember it like it was yesterday. It was a rainy night and I told him I wanted him to be my first. After contemplating whether I was making the right decision, one thing led to another, and we had sex.

At that moment, I didn't cherish or value my virginity. We remained intimate throughout our relationship. When I was younger, I would hear stories of how sex before marriage was wrong and how you're going to hell if you do it. But, I never understood why. Those close to me, never took the time to be *fully* transparent with me. So, I figured out the reality on my own.

At the age of 18, I felt like I was a grown woman and what I did with my body was my own business. Thus, my "first" became my first sexual soul tie. What is a sexual soul tie? When you engage sexually with someone, not only are you connecting to them physically and emotionally, but also spiritually. The more we had sex, the tighter the soul tie got. After our relationship ended abruptly, it was very hard for me to let go of him. Although we went our separate ways, and rarely saw each other, I couldn't get him out of my mind or my soul. If you think abstinence is tough, try breaking a sexual soul tie. He was still a part of me and I still felt connected to him. That was the beginning of my addiction.

CONFESSION NO. 4

When you're *single* and a *Christian*, it seems like fornication is considered the greatest of all transgressions. In God's eyes, a sin is a sin. However, often, "church folks" put sins on a hierarchy scale, ranking them according to what *they believe* produces the most shame. The church is supposed to be a place of healing and not of hindrance. It's supposed to be a place of redemption and not rejection. But, many people have been hindered and rejected in their growing walk with Christ, because they are constantly being judged and reminded of their past.

I've seen people's skeletons dragged out for everyone to see, while the accuser's issues remain tucked away in the back of their own closet. I've watched people pick and choose who are the sinners and who are the saints. I've sat in many congregations where I would see a single pregnant mother being judged because she had sex before marriage. I would overhear conversations, "If only she kept her legs closed," they would say. Time and time again, I saw these young women ridiculed for their decision to keep a child. Sometimes, "church folks" can be among the worst bullies when it comes to your journey of redemption.

I remember coming home from spring break during my Freshman year. As I was sitting in my mother's office browsing the internet, my email notification popped up. "You've got mail!" The subject line read: "For Brittany." Puzzled, because I didn't recognize the email address, I opened it anyway. As I read the message, I could feel my body sink into the chair. My eyes began to sting, and I could feel heavy waterfalls about to release. "You don't know who I am," the message began, "but I know who you are. You think you're all that, but you're not. You call yourself a Christian, but you are a hypocrite. God will never forgive you. You are nothing. You need to leave and never come back to this campus again."

I was stunned. I felt like someone had cut my chest open and left me to bleed. The saying, "Sticks and stones may hurt your bones, but words will never hurt you," is a complete lie. Hurting words do hurt. And, those words made me believe that I was worthless.

Little did the author know that prior to receiving this email, I had fasted and prayed to God for two weeks. Little did they know, I had re-dedicated myself to Christ and was working hard to build a better walk with Him. Little did they know, rather than healing me, their words hurt me to my core. Word of advice, what we say can affect someone's journey to their healing. We think by calling someone names or beating them over their head with their mistakes will put them on the right track. When in fact, it has the opposite impact. Negative, hurtful words only set people further back.

In that moment, I allowed their seed to grow in my heart. As they plainly wrote, and I unfortunately believed, God would never love me again. I believed that God would never forgive me again. I believed that I was nothing. I believed that, maybe, I should leave this college, and never return. These negative thoughts consumed me. I couldn't sleep at night. Who was this person writing such an awful email to me? Did anyone from the college know about this email?

The day before I was to return to campus, I opened the email again. As I read line after line, I began to cry out to God. I expressed my hurt, my pain, my fear, and my shame. I told God, "although I am being wrongfully judged, I will forgive that person, for they know not what they do."

Although I forgave the email's author, I still didn't have the strength to forgive myself. I didn't believe I was worth God's forgiveness or unconditional love. As I continued to question His love and forgiveness for me, I heard a loud voice sweep across the room. "Dry your eyes!" it commanded. Startled, I looked up, panning each corner of the room, but to my surprise, no one was there. Lowering my head, I heard the voice again. "Dry your eyes!"

"God?" I whispered. In that moment, God met me where I was. His love spoke to me and reminded me that, "Brittany, I've already forgiven you. No man can put you in heaven or hell. You are my beloved. Walk confidently in the restoration I have given unto you." If I didn't know before, I knew in that moment, that God loves me. That the validation of men cannot compare to God's redemptive power. From that moment, I walked with my eyes fixed on who God says I am and not what man says I am.

Scripture says, "for all have sinned, and come short of the glory of God" (Romans 3:23 KJV). I'll be the first to admit that I have sinned and come short of the glory of God. I haven't always dotted the Is or crossed the Ts or colored inside the lines like I was told I was supposed to. I looked for love of myself in men. I wanted to be my own healer and fill the rejection I felt inside. Even though I grew up in a home where I had parents who loved, adored, and took wonderful care of me, I still had insecurities and didn't love myself. Rejection was my sickness and being in a relationship was my medicine.

Sharing this story is part of my healing. Sharing this story is a form of my breakthrough. Too many of us are holding on to guilt and shame about the things we've done, about the things we've been through. Why be afraid to share the grace of God?

Maybe like me, you are afraid of what your family, accusers, friends, or your church might say? I know I was. I missed so many opportunities to minister about the way God's grace changed me because I felt condemned and guilty in the eyes of the people around me. For the sake of family, the church folks, and an email, I remained silent.

CONFESSION NO. 5

It was the winter of 2016 and my brothers and I were sitting in the living room. LJ was sprawled out across the couch rubbing his smooth, bald head. Gabe was stooped down on the stool checking his phone. And, I was sitting next to the fireplace admiring my two "heartbeats", my special nickname for my brothers.

We had just finished helping my parents around the house, and started laughing and talking about some of our childhood memories. One memory I recall, was my brothers bribing me to sign their test papers, so our parents wouldn't see their bad grades. Or, how we would build these huge clubhouses with our mother's nice, 800 thread count sheets. We all laughed and agreed, "Those were the days."

My brothers and I always shared a close bond. There was nothing that could ever separate us from the love we had for each other. We were each other's keepers and we kept each other's promises. But until that day, as close as we were in proximity, we never knew how close we were in pain.

As the laughter died down, we all got quiet. LJ yawned and stretched himself across the couch, laying his head on the pillow. Gabe grabbed his phone and went back to texting his friends. Since everyone was doing their own thing, I grabbed my phone and swiped through my Facebook feed. "What are you doing?" my mother said as she walked into the living room.

As my brothers were talking to her about women, out of the blue, my mother completely changed the subject and says to Gabe, "I hope you're still a virgin and that you will keep yourself until marriage." I kept scrolling through my phone, pretending not to hear the conversation. "Ma…I still am…and so is Britt…and LJ," Gabe said. I suddenly felt a sinking feeling of disappointment. Although I was now 29, it was as if I was 18 years old again. In that moment, I was Tessa. I felt I had disappointed myself, my family, and my God. Hot tears shot out of my eyes. I rushed to wipe them with the sleeves of my shirt hoping they wouldn't see, trying to discreetly mask my sniffles.

But, LJ's brotherly instincts immediately kicked in. Have you ever had the pressures of your past forced out of you? This was that moment for me. "What's wrong Britt," LJ asked. My Mom and Gabe immediately stopped talking. The three of them were all staring at me. I shook my head repeatedly, but my tears gave me away. "I haven't been honest with you guys," I began. Puzzled by my tears, LJ asked again, "What's wrong Britt?" "Did another guy hurt you?"

I shook my head, "No." "Well, what is it?" he asked again. Just like Tessa, I looked them in the eyes and said, "I haven't been perfect all my life. Your sister, made some bad decisions that I'm not proud of." I took a deep breath, "...But, I can't hold this secret in any longer. LJ and Gabe...I'm not a virgin. I lost my virginity when I was 18..."

Honey, I literally felt the weight of that secret fall off my shoulders onto my mother's living room floor the moment those words left my mouth. In that moment, I felt more liberated and unashamed and brave than I ever have in my life. Brave, for Tessa. Brave, for every person that has held a secret to keep from being judged. Brave, for me.

And to my surprise, instead of judging me as I feared they might, my brothers came running over to the chair where I sat and covered me. When I hurt, they hurt. When I laugh, they laugh. And, when I cry, they cry. And boy did we cry in each other's arms that day. "I'm sorry for disappointing you guys," I sobbed. "I was afraid to tell you because I didn't know what you would think of me." "No need to say sorry," they whispered in my ears, "You are not alone. We understand."

My brothers stood strongly with me. As we held each other, my Mother walked over and laid her hands on each of us. And, although I couldn't see her face, I felt every bit of her unconditional heart. Later that week, LJ called me and said, "Britt, thank you for being brave. You showed us that we can be brave too. You are a strong woman. And, we love you all the more for that." "Hey Britt, I think we need to celebrate this moment," Gabe hollered in the background, "so let's go out to eat! My treat!" My brothers always know how to put a smile on my face. After that phone call, God took a hold of my heart and told me these words, "Do not be silent anymore. There is no condemnation in Jesus Christ. I have forgiven you. Be my vessel and fulfill my glory."

I know I am not perfect. But through every mistake, I know I am redeemed. There are other Tessas and Brittanys out there who have not forgiven themselves. And, just like me, they have allowed people to hang a decade long necklace of mistakes around their necks. I had to come to terms with myself and decide that I would not allow people to dictate the direction or content of my testimony. I share my flaws openly now, because we all have them, and by doing so, I help bring healing to the body of Christ.

There are so many people waiting for the truth of your testimony, just like my brothers were waiting for mine. I encourage you to fight the attempt by anyone who wants to program your mind and make you believe that transparency is not a good and healthy thing. From the top of my lungs and the depths of my soul, my heart bellows to you, "Transparency is not embarrassing, it's necessary for healing!"

To all the prodigal daughters and sons, be of good courage. The world needs your stories and your truth. Your story will help others overcome their own struggles. Be the vessel God has called you to be. There are people out there that need to hear your voice. I am one of them.

PRAY ON PURPOSE

In James 5:15 it instructs us to, "Confess your faults one to another, and pray one for another, that ye may be healed. The effectual fervent prayer of a righteous man availeth much." I encourage you to be unashamed of your past. Don't look down on your flaws or the things you have done. You are here today because God brought you out of your past. You are alive today because He wants you to be a living testimony of what His grace looks like. Yes, you may have flaws, we all do, but God is a Redeemer who has covered us with His blood.

Repeat this: I have repented, and I am a new creature. I will walk in my renewal, and I will not look back. In Jesus' name, Amen.

8

TO LOVE ME OR NOT TO LOVE ME? THAT IS THE QUESTION

"And the very hairs on your head are all numbered. So don't be afraid; you are more valuable to God than a whole flock of sparrows." Luke 12:7 NLT

When we have strayed from His ways, God has a way of getting our attention. He wants us back in relationship with Him. He speaks and moves in unconventional ways. Sometimes it's through people, circumstances, places, or in this particular situation, a flat screen TV. That's right, God sent me a message via a television.

I remember it like it was yesterday, Walmart was having a pre-Black Friday sale and my mother wanted a new flat screen TV. "No problem," I said. "I'll buy it from the Walmart here. Then, when you and Dad come to visit me next weekend, you can pick it up then." I quickly hang up the phone with her and purchased the TV. It was a Saturday morning, and I called my then boyfriend, Luke, and asked if he could meet me there. I knew I wouldn't be able to lift the large TV into the car by myself.

After getting the hesitant *okay* with him, I called my mother to let her know that I had her TV. I told her that Luke was on the way to help me get it into the car. She sounded so excited. I knew she'd been waiting months to put a TV in her kitchen. I saw Luke pulling up in the parking lot behind me, "Mom, I'll call you back," I said, and I quickly tossed my phone into the passenger seat next to me.

"Hey Luke," I said. He gestures with a faint wave. It was clear that Luke arrived with an attitude and didn't want to be there. To keep the peace, I offered to help, grabbing one end of the large, awkward box, while he grabbed the other. As we tried to place the TV in the back of my car, it quickly became obvious that it wouldn't fit. "Ummm…I don't think this is going to fit," I said softly. He looked at me with disgust and proceeded to belittle me, "You're right stupid. Do you even know anything? You got me out here for nothing!"

"Don't talk to me like that," I said. But he continued. Unable to fit the TV in the car, he put down the box, turned, and stormed back to his car and sped away. Leaving me standing there alone in the parking lot. I had no idea what had prompted his outburst. But, it was not the first time he had spoken to me that way.

I climbed back into the front seat and grabbed my phone from where I had left it. I was upset and planned to call my friend to vent. I froze. Looking at the phone, I realized that my call to my mother had never disconnected, she was still on the line. "Hello…mom?" "Does he always talk to you like that?" she asked. "How long have you been going through this?" she demanded to know.

I quickly tried to defend Luke, "Mom, he's tired, he just got off from work." But, she wasn't buying it. "…No, no, no! That is unacceptable!" she said cutting me off, "What is going on Brittany?" I assured her all was well, that I had a Plan B and I would call her back.

PLEASE, TAKE ME WITH YOU

A week later, my parents arrived to pick up the TV. It was the first time they visited my chic college apartment in Harrisonburg, Virginia. At the time, I had three roommates. After introducing everyone, I insisted to take my parents out to dinner. We ate and talked for a few hours. I shared news about my classes and my plans for after graduation. We arrived back at my apartment after dinner to find it empty, my roommates had all left. Talk about divine timing!

My parents said they wished they could stay longer, but they had to get back home to some appointments the next morning. "Bye Britt," said my father as he kissed me goodbye and headed out to the car. "I love you Britt," said my mother as she hugged me and turned to follow my father down the walkway.

Suddenly, the thought of them leaving me sent a rush of anxiety washing over me. I literally dropped to my knees and begged, "Mom, please take me with you!" She turned to see me collapsed on the ground, sobbing, broken. I could no longer pretend that I was okay. I didn't want to spend another night in that apartment, in that town, I needed help.

My mother lifted me up and held me in her arms. "Baby, I know," she said softly, trying to console me, "God sent me here for this very reason. I'm not going to leave you." She walked me back inside, and helped me gather some clothes. I mindlessly stuffed them into my big black duffle bag along with some other things. All I knew for sure was that I was going home.

We walked outside to the car. My mother leaned into the window of my father's car, "She's riding home with us," she told him. I could see the look of concern in my father's eyes. But, he just nodded his head and said, "Okay." It was a long, three-hour ride home, but it was graceful. Grace met me, and grace brought me home. I let out a sigh of relief when we pulled into the driveway. My father grabbed my bag, and my mother and I walked into the house.

I headed straight up to my childhood room and collapsed on the bed. My mother sat beside me listening quietly as I told her everything. From the verbal abuse to the mental abuse. I even shared with her that we were sexually involved and I wanted to be free from every imaginable sexual soul tie.

I was sure my mother, the evangelist of the church, would judge and condemn me. But she didn't. She prayed with me and encouraged me that life would get better, reminding me that God can turn any situation around. Her unconditional love embraced my brokenness.

During this week, God rescued me from the misconception I had of myself. I thought that I had my life all figured out. But, my parents' timely visit showed otherwise. I thought I was just buying a television from Walmart. But really, my parents' visit was a reflection of how God is always on time with us. And, the 6-hour love sacrifice my parents made, was a reminder of how God unconditionally cares for us. It doesn't matter where we are and how much of a mess we've made, He will be there to rescue us.

As much as my heart wanted to rationalize why I should stay with Luke, my mind told me to leave. When you are on a brink of choosing happiness, it's amazing how your emotions and mind can be at war. I was in a constant battle with choosing me and my needs vs. choosing him and his. There were many times in the relationship where I told myself it was okay to put aside my own dreams and aspirations to support his. I loved Luke and I was willing to give up my happiness for him.

Since I was a little girl, I had always dreamed of working in communications and writing. I even had dreams of pursuing my Masters and Doctorate. And, moving to Los Angeles to pursue a career in the entertainment industry. But, Luke wanted to be a professional athlete. And, I was willing to throw away my dreams to be there for him. I made naive comments like, "I can always come back to my dreams later." I was so far into that man that I was willing to give up everything and move with him to wherever he signed a contract.

However, God saw otherwise. During that weekend at home with my family, I realized that I was choosing the wrong things. The wrong men. The wrong relationships. The wrong love. I was finding love in pain and not in purpose. I had one more semester before graduation and I had to make the decision to choose me. For so long, I chose Luke's needs over my own, and over God.

Like I said at the beginning of this chapter, God has a way of getting our attention when He wants us to get back into relationship with Him. It took a TV to wake me up from a toxic relationship. I was so focus on fulfilling Luke's purpose that I was neglecting my own, and as I watched my parents turn and walk away, I suddenly knew it. I had been willing to give up on my dreams and my future because I wanted to show Luke that I could support his sports career. I was using my hard earned money as a retail store clerk to take care of him. I was buying him shoes, clothes, gas, food, you name it. He was using me, and I knew it. But, I was too caught up in being "super-girlfriend." I was willing to do anything, even if it meant losing myself. But God took a television, and got me back on track. God did not want His daughter to be detoured from her purpose any longer. God stepped in, and like always He was right on time.

Do you know how valuable you are to God? Do you know how much He loves and adores you? You mean so much to Him that He will remove the wrong people out of your life. In fact, He will expose the situation you're in to get you out of it. He is the good shepherd and will do anything to keep His sheep safe. He is a good father. He is a protector of His children. It hurts Him to see His daughters and sons being taken advantage of and forgetting who they are.

My mother had been asking for months, "Is Luke treating you right? Is he abusive?" I would always cover up and say, "Yes he's treating me right. He's great to me." I thought by lying, I was proving my loyalty to Luke. But, what I should have been focused on was submitting my loyalty to God. It blows my mind every time I think of the goodness of God and how He brought me out of that situation. By using a TV, He restored me.

Before I got involved with Luke, I was confident, vibrant, courageous, strong-minded, and I was on fire for God. But after I met him, my insecurities all came screaming back. I struggled with depression, I felt weak minded, I did not love myself, and my relationship with God was unsteady at best.

I NEED SOMETHING MORE

It's amazing how one person can negatively impact your life if you allow it. When we lose our identity in a relationship, we expect the person we are dating to find it for us. One of the first signs that you are on the verge of losing your identity is when you lose sight of who you are and whose you are, and you find yourself compromising your standards and values. You choose to settle your standards rather than elevate your standards. In the Bible, Paul writes, "But I need something more! For if I know the law but still can't keep it, and if the power of sin within me keeps sabotaging my best intentions, I obviously need help! I realize that I don't have what it takes. I can do it, but I can't do it. I decide to do good, but I don't really do it; I decide not to do bad, but then I do it anyway. My decisions, such as they are, don't result in actions. Something has gone wrong deep within me and gets the better of me every time" (Romans 7:17-20 MSG).

Just like Paul, I found myself constantly going back into the same slump. Things I did not want to do, I found myself doing. The man I said I would not talk to again, I found myself calling. The relationship I did not want to settle in, I found myself settling. Thankfully, I eventually became tired of the continuous cycle of counterfeits and the baggage that continued to clutter my life. Instead of growing in the relationship, I felt like I was dying. It was not easy to break away from my ex. But one day, I had finally had enough. I made up my mind that I wanted to be happy. And you can make that same decision for yourself.

If you find yourself in a bad situation where you are not appreciated and valued, where you don't feel empowered to be your best self, I encourage you to choose you. When you choose you, you are telling the world that you love yourself. You begin to set boundaries and standards. If your partner can't honor those boundaries or standards, then they are not who God has for you. "I choose to love me," is a powerful statement. You are declaring that you choose happiness over pain. Joy over sorrow. Love over abuse. Freedom over fear. Peace over drama. When I chose to love me, God began to move quickly, powerfully, and miraculously in my life. I can truly say, He restored my heart, healed my body, gave me a new focus, and a new life.

PRAY ON PURPOSE

Dear God, teach me how to honor and protect my heart and my purpose. Teach me, God, to submit my all to you. Forgive me for lowering my standards and my values. Teach me to set Godly boundaries and give me the strength to protect them. Guard my heart against all counterfeits. Fix my eyes on you and the purpose you have for my life. I am determined that nothing shall separate me from the love of Christ. In Jesus' name, Amen.

9

WHAT MAKES YOU HAPPY?

"Sarah said, "God has made laughter for me; everyone who hears will laugh with me."" Genesis 21:6 NASB

Girls Trip! My friend, Angel and I were off to an all-inclusive resort in beautiful Cancun, Mexico. I was so excited for the white sand, private beaches, crystal blue waters, and delicious exotic foods…paradise was awaiting us. We were both looking forward to getting away from our stressful jobs…at least temporarily. It was going to be a much needed vacation for the both of us. Seven full days of rest, relaxation, and fun. Or, so I thought.

On day four, the phone rang. "How are you doing?" said my then boyfriend. "Let me get straight to the point. Do you think I am bad for you?" he asked. "Where is this coming from?" I said. The tone of his voice changed instantly, and he insisted that I answer his question. I hesitated, my mind was going 100mph. I started to panic:

"Was he having second thoughts about our relationship?"

"Did he cheat again while I was gone?"

"Does he feel like he is holding me back?"

"Is he trying to warn me about what was to come?"

Whatever it was, I wanted to find out. I quickly switched roles from girlfriend to an investigator. "Why are you asking me this question?" "Have you done something while I've been gone?" What was supposed to be a "friendly" conversation, quickly turned into an argument that ended in me hanging up on him.

The next morning the words, "Do you think I am bad for you?" continued to parade across my mind. I was literally speechless. But, I had to come to terms with the truth. I realized I was avoiding him, because I was afraid to give him a truthful response.

Little did he know, I had been keeping the truth inside for a long time. I didn't speak my truth because I didn't want to hurt his feelings or break his heart. Although he hurt mine in so many ways, still my heart was merciful towards his. I was afraid to tell him that, I was unhappy in the relationship. I was afraid to tell him that, I could not trust him any longer. I was afraid to tell him that, since I've been with him, I'd lost myself.

Later that evening, I stumbled on a book Angel was reading, *The Wait* by Devon Franklin and Meagan Goode. I asked her about it. After describing the key points, she suddenly stopped talking, looked at me for what felt like a long while and then asked, "Brittany, what makes you happy?"

I felt like I was on an episode of "Iyanla: Fix My Life." I realized I could not escape her or her question, just as I couldn't escape his question the night before on the phone. I just looked at her and stared. I didn't say anything.

I'm sure she could see the guilt in my eyes. But my "gift of gab" kicked in, and I just started talking, trying to distract her. But, I wasn't speaking from the heart. I was afraid to open up to her. I didn't want her to really see me. I didn't want her to know that I was truly unhappy in my relationship. For so long, I pretended that I was good, happy, whole, and healthy, and that everything in my life was perfect. I didn't want her, or anyone for that matter, to see that I was broken, confused, and unsure about who I was. I was going in circles and I knew she could see through me. And, if she could see through me, I knew the people back at home could see through me too.

PURSUING HAPPINESS

When was the last time you were truly happy? Do you even know what makes you happy? If you don't, right now is a great time to start on the path to getting to know yourself. Much like I did, some of you have lost your peace of mind. You are in a relationship where you are constantly worrying if the person you are with loves you for you or for what you can give them. I know from experience, if they don't love you now, they will never love you. You have to decide today to take back your happiness. There's nothing wrong with choosing your purpose over them. Life is too short to allow your purpose to pass you by. Your happiness and your peace of mind is more important than theirs. When you finally make the decision to pursue your happiness, never apologize for it. Never apologize for leaving an unhealthy relationship. The people I chose to be with in my past did not want to change. But, I wanted to.

But, I caution you. It won't be easy. In fact, the moment you decide to make a change to pursue your happiness the enemy will try and derail you. When I decided to pursue my own happiness, I received so much pushback. You think the people around you will be supportive, but often, they won't be.

The shade I experienced when I started making changes in my life was unreal. But, if I stayed in those unhealthy relationships, I would not be writing this book. I wouldn't be walking in my purpose today. I wouldn't be here to support you to be a better you.

Do not allow anyone to talk you out of becoming a better, healthier version of yourself. They'll talk, but don't you listen. Instead, I encourage you to keep walking in the direction of God and His happiness for your life.

If you find yourself bound to someone who is not right for you, who doesn't support you in becoming a healthier person, know that you deserve better. There's always a "FL;P" side to things. Don't let people's opinions trick you into thinking that you are wrong for pursuing your best self and your purpose.

I've wasted so much time worrying about the opinions of others. I stayed in relationships for years when I should've left. Yes, I wasted time, and you have wasted time, but God is a restorer and He always redeems the time. And, if He can restore me back to my rightful place, then He can do the same for you.

I am often asked, "What does being happy look like?" Here's 10 things God revealed to me:

1) Happiness is being free from every chain that has kept you bound.

2) Happiness is being liberated from your past guilt and shame.

3) Happiness is being able to rest peacefully. You are no longer tormented with thoughts of, "I wonder where they are?" or "I wonder who they are with?"

4) Happiness is having no regrets as you walk away from a toxic relationship. You realize it's not worth you losing your mind waiting for them to make up their mind.

5) Happiness is the ability to walk away from the opinions of others and to not listen to how they think your life should be. Being happy is a personal choice and it has nothing to do with naysayers.

6) Happiness is loving who you are as a person and not compromising your well-being for the sake of keeping someone.

7) Happiness is knowing that you are healthy in your mind, body, heart, and soul. You are committed to your well-being and will maintain it at any cost.

8) Happiness is listening to your heart. When you are happy, you are in tune with your heart and you pursue the things that you love.

9) "You look happier," is the greatest compliment you can receive. Continue to let your happiness shine above the pain of your past.

10) Happiness is being fearless to new beginnings, new careers, new vibes, new environments, new paths, new levels, new people, and new challenges. Your happiness will not allow you to dwell in the past. Why? The past is a place of reference and not a place of residence.

PRAY ON PURPOSE

Dear God, teach me your perfect happiness. I want to live a healthy and happy life. I want to have a healthy heart and mind. What is not good for me, please remove those things. Allow me to block out the opinions of others and hear only your voice. I choose to be happy. I choose my purpose. I thank you for allowing me to see that I am nothing without You. Continue to be my guide as I walk through this journey of happiness. In Jesus' name, Amen.

10

TABLE FOR ONE, PLEASE!

"She has prepared her food, she has mixed her wine; She has also set her table." Proverbs 9:2 AMP

"Hello, welcome to Outback. Table for two?" The hostess greeted me as I walked in. "No mam," I said, with a huge smile on my face, "Just one." "Would you like to go to the bar?" she asked. "No," I replied, still smiling, "I prefer a table." She looked at me awkwardly, grabbed a menu, and led me to a table. I was hoping she wouldn't seat me in a corner or at the back of the restaurant like they so often do when you are dining alone. I was happy that she placed me front and center in the midst of all the other diners.

I noticed people turn their heads to look as I sat down. I *nodded and smiled* and put my napkin on my lap. "Geesh…have you never seen a young woman eat by herself?" As I reviewed the menu, my waitress approached me. "Hi, my name is Amy. I will be your server." Like the hostess, she asked, "Are you expecting anyone else?" "No just me," I said, smiling. "You're brave," she said. "I wish I could do that." "You can," I replied. "It's not hard as you think."

To others, it may have looked like I was alone, but I knew I was not. For the first time in my life, I was beginning to feel comfortable in my own skin. I was at peace, and the people around me could see that. I was truly walking in my happiness. There was a time when dining by myself would've been impossible. I was too afraid to ever go out and eat alone, or anywhere by myself. I was the kind of person who always needed someone to accompany me wherever I went. Why? I was afraid to learn what being alone would feel like.

When I finally decided to be single again, I was determined that this time, rather than finding another man, I would date myself. I was going to take the time to learn about who I was and how to love me. No interruptions, no fill in the gaps, no let me test the waters with this one or that one --- in this season I chose to embrace the gift of singleness.

For so long, I searched for men to love and adore me. But, how could I expect them to do that when I didn't even love myself. You would think a 28-year-old woman would have known what loving herself looked like. But, I didn't. However, this time I made a vow to my heart to learn me first, before I expected anyone else to get to know me.

So, how did I do that?

First, by communing with God. Who knows you better than Him? He knows every hair on your head. He knows your genetic makeup. He is the Creator. When I began to take time with God, He began to teach me about myself. I learned that my identity was fashioned in Christ. When I began to fashion myself in God's Word, I began to tap into His love. When I began to pray, God began to open my eyes to my purpose.

In my daily devotions, God showed me how to be one with Him. He placed me in a season of quietness. There I began to reflect on why certain relationships didn't work out. By taking the time to look back, I saw that God was not imprisoning me, but preserving me for my purpose.

When you have a calling on your life, when you have been chosen by God; you cannot be with just anyone. God has designed you for that special man or woman who will not only support your purpose, but protect it. Anyone outside of His will is a counterfeit.

God knew that I had to write this book. God knew that He would use me to minister to the lost and broken. God knew He had to get me to a place of loving myself so I could teach others how to love themselves. How could I teach you how to love yourself and find your purpose, if I didn't know my own?

God has a perfect plan for your life. I encourage you to accept His Plan and not neglect it. If the relationship does not work out, don't worry, let that man or woman go! They were not designed for you in the first place. Be happy that God is leading you one step closer to the purpose He has for you.

Second, date yourself. There is nothing wrong with being single. I encourage you to go out to places by yourself. Learn what you like and what you don't like. How can you expect someone to date you, and give you what you want and need, when you don't even know what that is? Don't let people make you feel like you are crazy and depressed because you prefer to go out alone. Taking time with yourself is important for learning who you are.

There's nothing wrong with catering to the queen or king that is inside of you. I started going to the movies by myself, on dinner dates by myself, even traveling the world by myself. The more I catered to me, the more I appreciated my worth. I was determined to not settle for anything less than what I knew God wanted for me. And, I held on to my values of faith, self-worth, unconditional love, honesty, and courage at the same time.

Lastly, learn how to accept the exit. When God gives you a way out, do not turn back, take it. So many of us pray to God, "If you get me out of this relationship, I won't go back." Then God gets us out. But, instead of walking through the exit, we continue to stay in the room of unhappiness. If God gives you the opportunity to move, go! There were many times that God created exits for me. But, I refused to walk through them. In the long run, I ended up hurting myself and delaying the things God had waiting for me.

You are too beautiful and valuable to be walked on like a doormat or hurt by anyone. Embrace the gift of the exit. Just as God creates an entry way, He also creates an exit way. When

God tells you to leave an unhealthy relationship, know that He has something better for you. A lot of times we stay because we feel that we cannot get anything better. Trust me, God never makes a mistake when He instructs you to take the exit. Trust God and have faith in His direction. Don't look at the exit as a loss, but as a gain. When I did that, I realize that His exit, is a gateway to a better door.

PRAY ON PURPOSE

This is the day that the Lord has made, I will rejoice and be glad in it! Today marks a new beginning to loving yourself. God, I accept the season to walk alone. In this season, teach me to love myself and learn myself. Teach me to be obedient and to accept the beauty of the exit. In Jesus' name, Amen.

Part III

What does **I.N.** mean?

In this section, we will discuss how we sometimes "**Internalize Negativity**." There are so many roots of insecurities that we are not aware of. We have kept these insecurities hidden for so long. These insecurities have clouded our purpose, our vision, our happiness, and our peace. When you lack confidence in yourself, you make yourself believe that it is impossible to move forward. Do not allow your insecurities to run you. Do not allow your insecurities to break you. This section will teach you how to purge those insecurities from the inside out.

11

WELL-NESS CHECK

"Jesus replied, "If you only knew the gift God has for you and who you are speaking to, you would ask me, and I would give you living water." John 4:10 NLT

Each year, I schedule an appointment with my doctor to have my physical. Because I am a big advocate on health and wellness, it is imperative that I be in the know about my body. I consider myself a healthy person. I workout 2-4 times a week, eat "pretty" healthy, and take my multivitamins. Sounds pretty healthy, wouldn't you agree?

But, in 2015, I had a huge wake up call. I arrived at the doctor's office a few minutes early. "Ms. Brooks, come with me," said the nurse, and I followed her down the long hall to the examining room. She instructed me to, "Have a seat. The doctor will be with you shortly."

I felt pretty confident that I would receive a good report. After waiting about five minutes, the doctor stepped in. "Hi Ms. Brooks, good to see you again. Well, you know the routine. I will read your results, and if you have any questions please let me know." She sat down and opened her laptop and began to read my test results line by line.

"Everything looks good for the most part, except one area. Your vitamin D levels seem to be extremely low." "How low is low?" I asked. She turned the screen toward me and pointed to the level it should be then slowly moved her finger down the page to where I currently was. All I could say was, "Wow."

I asked her about the importance of vitamin D and the symptoms of having this deficiency. "Vitamin D is important for your body because it contributes to bone growth and protects you against cancer," she explained. "If your levels are low, you are at risk for developing bone abnormalities." She continued, "You might also experience fatigue, depression, mood swings, hair loss, headaches, muscle pain, and so on." I sat there listening, in complete shock. "I will prescribe you some supplements to help raise your levels," she said. Without hesitation I agreed. I left the doctor's office with a prescription in hand, realizing that I didn't have it all together as I thought. I wasn't taking care of my body like I should be. I was pretending to be healthy, when I really wasn't.

When it comes to your well-being, there are four areas that matter most: your heart (emotional), your soul (spiritual), your body (physical), and your mind (mental). You cannot operate efficiently or effectively if either of the four are ill. For example, there are people who have a healthy body, but are not healthy in their mind and heart. There are people who have their spiritual life intact, but their body is in a health scare. How can you operate effectively in your purpose, when you are not taking care of yourself? Externally, it might appear that you have it all together, but if your internal life is a mess, do you really have it together like you say you do?

Consider a familiar story from the Bible, the woman at the well (John 4 NLT). Like most of us, she perceived her life to be content. That is, until she visited the well. She did not schedule an appointment. However, Jesus saw fit to make a destiny appointment with her. She approached the well and found Him there waiting. He asked her for a drink and she looked at Him in disbelief. In those times, Samaritans and Jews were not even supposed to speak to one another. In addition, men were not permitted to engage in conversation with a woman unless her husband was present.

But, Jesus made a grace exception. The woman at the well was focused on the law, but Jesus came to her in Love. "If you only knew the gift God had for you and who you were speaking to, you would ask me, and I would give you living water." She asked Him questions about where to get this living water, and how this water was better than the water she already had. She insisted that Jesus give her this water. But He replied, "Go and get your husband."

"I don't have a husband," she said. Jesus replied, "You're right! You don't have a husband— for you have had five husbands, and you aren't even married to the man you're living with now. You certainly spoke the truth!"

Like the woman at the well, many of us live two separate lives to please two different types of people. To please the spectators, we try to appear that we are living our best life. We wear the finest clothes and we post images of every event we attend on social media. When people look at your page you portray someone who is happy with your life, at peace with yourself, and winning with your "Bae goals." However, behind closed doors, your life is a struggle.

Here's a newsflash! God sees what "your followers" cannot see. God sees how you spent your last dime to keep up with the trends. God sees that you are far from peace, that your body is tired, and your mind is weary. Just like the woman at the well, He sees that you are dry and in need of the living water. God sees the constant arguments that you have with "Bae." He sees that you are unfulfilled, unhappy, and are being held captive in an unpromising relationship. But, why do we often become more comfortable in captivity than freedom?

I will tell you from experience, we tend to hang on to the people that are the most familiar to us, even when that means hanging on will cause more hurt, discomfort, and pain. Having never experienced the joy of freedom and the peace in love, we don't know what it looks like or feels like. The unknown is scary for most of us. We say we want to be free, but in our mind we want to be trapped. Why? Oftentimes, our familiarity eases our discomfort. And somehow, we will choose unpromising people to fulfill a promising relationship.

For instance, we say we desire a God-fearing man, one that will treat us like a queen and adore us, a man that has his life fully together, but we stay with counterfeits. Listen! Whatever mindset you're cultivating, that's what you're going to attract. If you cultivate a mindset that is okay with dating beneath your standards, then you will attract men who are beneath your standards.

Men, this concept applies to you too. You say you desire a God-fearing woman who is loyal. A driven woman who fulfills her goals. A woman who will honor and respect you. But then, you go out with women who are the opposite.

And please be clear. A ring and a walk down the aisle will not change anything. If someone acts a certain way when you are dating them, then that's how it will be when you're married to them, if not much worse.

God saw that the woman at the well was living beneath her potential, constantly thirsting after relationships that were not fulfilling her. He was letting her know that He had the solution to her thirst. He was letting her know she was in need of a "Well-ness" check. He wanted her to know that He could quench her thirst. He was the solution to all the pain she was experiencing.

If you are in an unhealthy relationship, but are still trying to convince yourself that you have it all together, trust me when

I say, I've been in your shoes. I've been involved in so many situations where I was with someone, but my heart still felt widowed, alone, and empty. But one day, God met me at my own well. He showed me that I don't have to use relationships to fill a void. He showed me that I don't have to lower my standards to have a man. He showed me that I don't have to be a prisoner to my pain. I challenge each of you to stop subjecting yourself as a prisoner. There's a palace outside of the prison that you are living in, you just have to decide if you want to live there.

PRAY ON PURPOSE

God, I am ready to be filled with your living water. No longer do I want to thirst after unhealthy relationships. No longer do I want to thirst after the wrong things. I long to thirst after a relationship with you. I desire to thirst after your righteousness.

I pray that you fill every void in my life with the Fruit of the Spirit. God fill me with your love, joy, peace, self-control, patience, kindness, goodness, faithfulness, and gentleness. God, I desire an overflow in every area of my life. In Jesus' name, Amen.

12

RESIDUE

"Jesus said unto him, Let the dead bury their dead: but go thou
and preach the kingdom of God." Luke 9:60 KJV

I was attending my friend's book release party when my ex
walked through the front door. I tried to ignore his presence
and continue talking with my friends, but my heart was
distracted. Not just by him, but by the painful memories I still
had of our relationship. I had convinced myself that the painful
emotions were buried and gone, but after seeing him, I knew
that they weren't.

All of the anger and frustration that I thought was gone,
started to rise up in me. The women he cheated on me with
(women I thought were erased from my mind), were popping
up into my mind. It was clear from my reaction that God was
showing me that there was still residue in my life. The residue

of mistrust. The residue of anger. The residue of pain. The residue of unforgiveness. And, the residue buildup was heavier and deeper than I ever imagined.

Residue is something that remains after the main part is gone. After we ended our relationship, I assumed all the pain was gone. I was wrong. Just because the person isn't in your life anymore, doesn't mean the hurt and the memories go with them. Pharaoh was gone, but that didn't mean the bondage mentality left the Israelites. God was showing me that I was still bound to the residue.

After my reaction to seeing him, I knew I still had some healing to do. To get rid of the residue I literally embarked on a spiritual detox of my mind, heart and soul. I followed five steps to clear myself of that past hurt and disappointment:

1) *I Created a Breakthrough List.* Before I started my spiritual detox, I created what I call a "Breakthrough List." This list consisted of writing down what I wanted God to do in my next season. I divided the paper in half. On one side, I listed the types of residue I wanted God to purge from me. Things like (but not limited to): soul ties, insecurity, distrust, anxiety, bitterness, rejection, anger, unforgiveness, guilt, fear, disappointment, resentment, condemnation, and hurt. Then, I wrote down the names of all the people that had hurt me. On the other side of the page, I listed what I wanted God to restore back to me. I wrote down things like a clean heart, forgiveness, a

renewed mind, a contrite spirit, joy, peace, love, faith, a new focus, and a stronger relationship with God.

2) *I Fasted.* I really wanted God to break the strongholds of bondage over my life. So, I scheduled a weekly fast. I recommend catering your fast to what God wants you to do. I asked God for guidance and He instructed me to do the Daniel Fast. The Daniel Fast consisted of eating only fruits, nuts, seeds, and vegetables. And, avoiding dairy, sweets, sodas, meats, and breads.

3) *I Devoted Myself to Scripture.* I sought scriptures to read and meditate on them every day. Psalm 51, Galatians 5, Matthew 5, Matthew 6, Psalm 1, Romans 8, Ephesians 6, and Psalm 139 were my weekly devotionals.

4) *I Prayed.* I prayed over my "Breakthrough List" every day. This is the most intimate place you can be. It's just you and God. I set aside time to pray in the morning and in the evening.

5) *I Read Books.* I searched for literature on destiny and purpose. Some of my favorite books were TD Jakes' *Destiny,* Christine Caine's *Undaunted,* and Sarah Jakes Roberts' *Lost and Found.* I highly recommend immersing yourself in inspirational literature to help get your mind focused.

On your journey to healing and freedom, the enemy will constantly test your commitment to your purpose. He will use anything to distract you, trying to get you back into that place of bondage. How can God move you to the next level in your life, when you are still bound? Sometimes we allow residue to get us off track. In Matthew 8:22, Jesus told a man to follow him. However, the man told Jesus he would follow him later because he wanted to bury his father. Jesus responded, "let the dead bury their own dead" (Matthew 8:22 NIV).

Sounds pretty harsh, right? Why would Jesus not allow the man to bury his father? To see his father one last time?

There are times when we will make every excuse to not follow Christ and do what He has told us to do. We will use our residue as an excuse for not moving to the next level. We desire that last fix. As the old folks say, "we want to test the waters." We get caught up with thoughts like, "I wonder if he still wants me?" The next thing you know, you are calling him in the middle of the night, sleeping with him, and opening doors that should remain closed.

I'll admit, it was extremely hard for me to let go of one particular man. There were times where I felt like I was moving on with my life and I wouldn't answer his calls and texts. But 24 hours later, I'd find myself texting him back. Then 48 hours after that, we'd be back together.

Have you ever tried to be hard with a someone who has hurt you, but you still have a soft heart towards them? That was me. There were times when I would meet him for lunch or talk to him on the phone when I should've been doing something else. I knew God had told me to cut ties with this guy, but I would come up with every excuse to justify seeing him. I would say things like, "God, I need to forgive him and let him know how I feel in person." Or, "God he wants to talk in person. So…we are going to have a simple lunch." Or, "God your Word teaches us to forgive and to love one another. So…I am going to show him love." Here's a newsflash! The only closure you need is understanding that you deserve better. However, we will find every excuse to justify why we should go back:

"Well, I never got full closure."

"It wouldn't hurt if I text back."

"Now that I think about it, the relationship wasn't that bad."

I understand why Jesus told the disciples that they didn't have time for distractions because their purpose was far more important. Forms of residue will pop up and try to distract you on your journey to freedom. But you have the power to say, "No!" You have the power to say, "Enough is enough!"

We will easily negotiate our purpose and trade our values just to have one last night with our addiction. We would rather be around dead things than the true living one, God. But, God has not given us the spirit of fear, but rather a spirit of love, power, and a sound mind. It's time to take control. Tell the enemy that he will not have your mind. He will not bring condemnation, guilt or things of the past to haunt you. You are a child of the King, which makes you heir to God's love.

I challenge you to wipe the residue from your heart, mind, and soul. You must make up your mind that residue shall not move you anymore. God is calling us to leave the things behind that don't complement His will and press towards what is ahead.

PRAY ON PURPOSE

Dear God, purify my heart and mind from all residue. I desire to stay on my journey to freedom. Help me to stay the course. Block all distractions sent from the enemy to keep me away from my purpose. Give me a determined mind to focus on your will and not on my own. Remove all baggage from my life. In Jesus' name, Amen.

13

BEATY FOR ASHES

"David noticed that his attendants were whispering among
themselves, and he realized the child was dead. "Is the child
dead?" he asked. "Yes," they replied, "he is dead." Then David
got up from the ground. After he had washed, put on lotions
and changed his clothes, he went into the house, of the Lord
and worshipped. Then he went to his own house, and at his
request they served him food, and he ate."
2 Samuel 12:19-20 NIV

Have you ever felt like you don't deserve God's mercy and

grace? Better yet, have you ever felt like you could never forgive

yourself for all of your sins? Do you feel like a failure after you

have come short of God's glory? Well, I have. The truth is, my

skeletons could fill every closet in my house and possibly yours

too.

There was a time in my life when I was a total wreck from

the inside out. My mind was set on the notion that there was no more hope for me. I thought all of the chances given to me had expired. But God is a God of grace and mercy. He is truly a God of a second, third, and ninety-ninth chance.

Regardless of what you have done, how many mistakes you constantly make, or the number of disappointments you carry with you, God's forgiveness is unconditional.

The story of David reminds us of God as a Redeemer to the broken. David was a mighty man of God, yet, he had so many flaws. He loved God, but he battled with so many struggles, including lust. These lustful struggles opened doors to deceit, adultery, and even murder.

And just like David, I had so many struggles that I felt I could never free myself from. To anyone who has battled with lust, hurt, depression, anxiety, guilt, fear, insecurities, suicidal thoughts, or feelings of rejection, you too can be set free. I am alive to tell you that whatever your situation is, God can turn it around for your good.

Your life may seem dry, dirty, or even desolate. However, God can still make all things new. He is the Creator of all things, therefore He can create a miracle out of your dead situation. I am a living witness that God can turn your mourning into dancing...your pain into purpose...your shame into success.

How can God do that?

Part of your healing is truly knowing that you are forgiven. We are so focused on beating ourselves down for the things that we have done, that we neglect to see the beauty of God's forgiveness. When God tells you that there is no condemnation in Him, believe it. People may remind you of your failures, but when God forgives you, you are not bound to people's opinions or your past mistakes and setbacks. In fact, the Bible says, "Once again you will have compassion on us. You will trample our sins under your feet and throw them into the depths of the ocean" (Micah 7:19 NLT).

Regardless of what you do, you can never escape God's unconditional love. No matter what mistakes you make, I encourage you to forgive yourself as He does.

It's often easier to forgive others than it is to forgive ourselves. For me, I felt like I didn't deserve forgiveness. I felt like I couldn't repay God back for all the things I had done. I allowed the enemy to make me feel that God would never forgive someone like me. I felt I had constantly let God down and failed to keep my promises of staying committed and pure before Him. I felt unworthy.

I became so *damaged* and *broken* on the inside, that I no longer *recognized* who I was out in the world. My feelings of depression and rejection were so deep, I believed no remedy could cure them.

GRACE'S TABLE

It was an unusually cold day in March. I was a sophomore home from college for Spring Break. It was supposed to be a time of fun and relaxation. And, enjoying time off from school, studying, tests, and deadlines. However, I was depressed and convinced that life couldn't offer me anything. I felt dead on the inside and I was willing to make that feeling a reality. At that time in my life, I felt so covered in the ash of lust, abuse, and rejection that I was afraid to walk in the church. I was afraid people would judge me as I saw them judge others. There were times that I felt like my life was not worth living. I felt like I had let my mother down, my father down, my brothers, and all of the people that looked up to me.

I decided to end it all. I poured my heart into a suicide note, writing of my shame, guilt, and regret of not being the perfect Christian or the perfect daughter. I wrote of my many mistakes, one weighing heavily on me was losing my virginity and how I longed for forgiveness and acceptance.

I put the note on the kitchen table, got a knife from the drawer by the dishwasher and then called my mother at her job. "I am sorry for all I've done," I told her. "I don't want to live anymore." I could feel my mother's heartbeat pound loudly over the phone. "Brittany, stay on the phone with me. You hear me? Please baby. I am on my way! Stay with me." My mother continue to talk to me on the phone. To her, ending the call meant ending her child's life and she couldn't bare the thought of losing me. My mother's office was five minutes from the house. I could imagine how five minutes felt like five hours to her. Frantic, my mother immediately calls a three-way with my father at his job. I could hear the uneasiness in my father's voice, "I'm coming now!" and hangs up the phone. She burst through the front door to find me sitting at the bottom of the staircase holding a knife. With tears in my eyes, I told her, "What can God do with a mess like me?"

"Give me the knife baby," she said calmly, "It's not worth it." I was reluctant at first, but then a touch of mercy moved my hand to hers. She carefully took the knife out of my hand, tossed it on the floor, and scooped me up in her arms. Moments later, my father appeared at the front door. I could tell he had been praying to God, I saw the concern on his face and his eyes were watered with emotion.

He didn't ask me any questions, he just told me to come sit with him at the kitchen table. Reaching for his work bag, he pulled out a thick black book, placed it on the table, and slide it in front of me. "Open it," he said calmly.

The thick black book was my father's Bible. He instructed me to turn to different scriptures and read each one aloud:

1) I can do all things through Christ which strengtheneth me (Philippians 4:13 KJV).

2) For You formed my inward parts; You covered me in my mother's womb. I will praise You, for I am fearfully and wonderfully made; Marvelous are Your works, And that my soul knows very well (Psalm 139:13-14 NKJV).

3) How precious also are Your thoughts to me, O God! How great is the sum of them! If I should count them, they would be more in number than the sand; When I awake, I am still with You (Psalm 139:17-18 NKJV).

4) The Lord will guide you continually, And satisfy your soul in drought, And strengthen your bones; You shall

be like a watered garden, And like a spring of water, whose waters do not fail (Isaiah 58:11 NKJV).

5) Casting all your care upon Him, for He cares for you (1 Peter 5:7 NKJV).

6) For God so loved the world that He gave His only begotten Son, that whoever believes in Him should not perish but have everlasting life. For God did not send His Son into the world to condemn the world, but that the world through Him might be saved (John 3:16-17 NKJV).

7) Finally, brethren, whatever things are true, whatever things are noble, whatever things are just, whatever things are pure, whatever things are lovely, whatever things are of good report, if there is any virtue and if there is anything praiseworthy – meditate on these things (Philippians 4:8 NKJV).

As I read, the words confirmed to me that I was created for a purpose driven destiny. In those hours sitting with my father, God introduced me to His grace and love. It was one of the most beautiful things that I ever experienced.

In God's grace and love, you are free from the opinions of others. In God's grace and love, you are redeemed by the blood of the Lamb. God gently reminded me that, "It is of the Lord's mercies that we are not consumed, because his compassions fail not (Lamentations 3:22-23 KJV)," and by knowing that, I was able to embrace his forgiveness fully.

I encourage you to do the same. Stop judging yourself and allowing the opinions of others to keep you from walking in full forgiveness. Lay aside every depression and suicidal thought. As my father reminded me that day, so I remind you, you were created with purpose. God loves you my dear and you don't have to condemn yourself for what has happened in your past. God doesn't look at you and think, "You are a hot mess. You are useless." Instead God says, "Watch me use their brokenness for my glory."

I overcame the guilt of my past, and so can you. I am a living witness, that God can turn your ashes into beauty. If God can forgive me, what makes you think he cannot forgive you? I encourage you to walk in your forgiveness and embrace His love every day.

PRAY ON PURPOSE

Dear God, you are such a loving and merciful God. Thank you for loving me in spite of all my flaws. I pray that you teach me this same love. To not walk in unforgiveness of myself, but to forgive me. I embrace your love and grace. I pray that you enter my heart and renew me of all the pain I experienced in my past.

God, I want you to break every stronghold of suicide, depression, oppression, rejection, and loneliness. Wrap me with your loving arms. I want to be free from the chains of my past.

Every negative and toxic thought that infiltrates my mind, I cast it down in the name of Jesus! I shall not walk with my head down, but I shall walk in this confidence: "So if the Son sets you free, you will be free indeed" (John 8:36 NIV). Thank you for this new chapter of my life. I embrace the newness that you have given me with my whole heart. In Jesus' name, Amen.

14

OBEDIENCE IS BETTER THAN SACRIFICE

"But Samuel replied, What is more pleasing to the Lord: your burnt offerings and sacrifices or your obedience to his voice? Listen! Obedience is better than sacrifice, and submission is better than offering the fat of rams." 1 Samuel 15:22 NLT

When you have been hurt in a relationship you always have two choices: choose to stay or choose to leave. Raise your hand if you've ever chosen to stay in a relationship where you weren't respected or treated like the Queen or King that you are, in hopes of making it work? I know I have.

There were times when an ex-boyfriend hurt me to my core, but over and over again, I would take him back. All he had to do was say, "I am sorry," give me those puppy dog eyes, maybe shed a tear or two, and we were back together. I fell for this game each and every time. That is, until I finally woke up and saw the truth of what it was. Truth hurts, but the truth will save you, the truth will set you free.

Early one Monday morning, I found out I was being cheated on. Is there anything worse than finding out you've been cheated on while on your way to work? Can I get an Amen? I was heading out the door when my friend Michelle called me. "Girl...you won't believe what I found out?"

"What's up Michelle?" I said, feeling a bit impatient. "I know you hate to hear this," she said, "but you need to let go of that man. He's messing with his ex again." At first, I didn't believe her. Michelle is the type to know everyone else's business, but refuses to speak of her own. But then she gave me the details on who it was and how long he had been messing with his old girlfriend. I couldn't just shake it off. I knew she was telling the truth because for months my womanly intuition was on high alert. On top of that, God sent me dreams, visions, and signs to open my eyes. But, I would ignore them and keep it moving. I would convince myself that maybe I was paranoid and overthinking this thing. I would convince myself it would work, but in the end, I eventually got hurt yet again...and again and again.

Sometimes we allow our emotions to lead us rather than God. We allow our flesh to override God's plan for our lives. The Bible speaks of how obedience is better than sacrifice. I neglected the obedience to God by staying with my ex. I took him back because I did not trust what God was showing me and I did not want to accept the truth He was speaking to me.

We sometimes sacrifice our relationship with God for the sake of being with someone. When I took my ex back, it was an act of sacrifice and not an act of obedience. I eventually realized I was so busy wanting to take him back, when I should have been focusing on getting myself back. I finally realized, "I should have never left me!" We can easily lose ourselves in unhealthy relationships. We throw away our power, our self-love, our integrity, and our purpose to be with someone. We allow them to change our lives, not for the better, but for the worse. I've seen it happen over and over again.

Let's take this common scenario. You are driven. You are focused on your purpose. You value and uphold your standards and your boundaries. Then you meet someone. That someone tells you what you want to hear. And, after a while, you go from loving yourself to losing yourself. You compromise your standards and remove your boundaries. You lose your identity. All because you want someone to fill your empty void. That someone gets what they want. That someone breaks your heart. In the end, you are *physically, emotionally, mentally, and spiritually depleted.* You were emptier than you were before.

This happens time and time again. We will invest so much time and energy into someone to the point that we lose sight of investing time and energy in ourselves. We put our lives and dreams on hold because we desire that picture perfect "Love." We assume that what we see on Instagram, Facebook, or reality TV is real, and the "Bae" we want, is the one we are willing to lose ourselves to get. We accept the world's conditions of love

110

rather than God's conditions. We will give up ourselves to settle for less. We will subject ourselves to love triangles. We will drink the magic potion and convince ourselves, "If I stay, they will eventually come to their senses and choose me." We will dress ourselves in the false impression of love, and sometimes to the point that we worship these very beliefs:

"Verbal abuse is okay - as long as they don't hit me, right?"
"At least they come home to me, right?"

We stay with a person that is a liability versus being with a person who is an asset. A person who has characteristics of a liability constantly brings fears, threats, conflicts, distractions, stressors, inconsistencies, sorrows, injuries, insecurities, and depletions in the relationship. However, a person that is an asset produces growth, gives solutions, gives security, yields a return, produces happiness, brings value, and adds purpose to the relationship.

LIABILITY VS. ASSET

I can recall a time when I was dating this guy. I was head over hills for him. One evening, as I got home from a date, I asked my father, "How do you feel about him?" My father was quiet for a minute. Thinking he didn't hear me, I repeated the question. "Dad! So what do you think about my new beau?" My father raises from his chair, stands firm, and looks over at me

111

and says, "Brittany, when God blesses you with a gift, he adds no sorrow." Baffled by his response, I asked my father, "What does that mean, can you speak plainly for me? Dad, do you like him or no?" Without hesitation, my father repeats, "When God blesses you with a gift, he adds no sorrow." At that point, I didn't know what to say, so I closed the door behind me and went to my room. My father is a man of few words and he tends to speak in riddles. However, what my father said in that moment profoundly stuck with me. Without any thought of the consequences, I pursued the relationship anyway. As I was three months into dating, I begin to understand what my father meant. The guy that I was talking to, constantly kept me in tears. Whether it was finding out he was cheating or breaking my self-esteem, my happiness was depleting. I found myself more mentally, spiritually, physically, and emotionally drained with having to maintain a level of comfort in the relationship. Word of advice, you will always find love drowning if you date people you have to raise. I was forcing peace in the relationship. Ladies, there was no peace, but constant sorrow!

When God blesses you with that perfect mate, he is blessing you with an asset and not a liability. God knows the difference of who will add value and who will deplete you. I ignored my father's wisdom and followed my own path. I sacrificed staying with the guy versus being obedient to what God was pouring into my father at that time. How many times have your parents told you about someone not worthy of your value? How many times have a friend or a loved one expressed how that "liability" will hurt you in the long run? It is important to know that when you are blind to see your mess, that God will give His eyes to your parents, friends, and loved ones. I encourage you to not ignore the wise counsel of those God has placed in your life. They are not here to hurt you, but to help guide your heart.

The truth is, being with a liability is not okay. In fact, it is destructive. It is destructive to your heart, mind, body, and soul. Time after time, I've watched young ladies willingly accept a "partial love" rather than accepting what love was created to be, whole. Yes, we all want to be loved. Yes, we were all created to love. But God also created us to wait. In your season of waiting in obedience, I pray that God prepares you to be an asset. Ask God to teach you how to be of value and of growth to the relationship He has predestined for you. Remember, God has already set aside your purpose mate. Therefore, continue to seek God, seek His righteousness, and remain obedient to His will. As you stay connected in God and His will for your life, He will keep your heart from relationships that are liabilities. Remember, falling in love with someone is great, but loving yourself first is far better.

PRAY ON PURPOSE

Heavenly Father, teach me to walk in your obedience. Teach me your will and your way. I surrender my heart to you. I surrender my mind to you. I surrender my all to you. I pray that you will lead me in every way and that my emotions will not lead me. Lord, I will not turn away from the things you have shown me.

God keep my heart from all evil. Keep me away from anything that will taint my purpose. Keep me away from liabilities. Keep me away from the very things that will redirect my steps. Father, I want you to align my heart with your Word. Father, teach me to be obedient to your voice. Open my ears to hear your instructions. Open my eyes to see your path. In Jesus' name, Amen.

Part IV

What does **P.U.R.P.O.S.E.** mean?

We will discover seven areas in this section: **Position, Unlock, Resource, Preparation, Opportunity, Strategy, and Execution.** Now, that we have learned from our lessons, we will take those lessons and build them into purpose. Remember, your breakup doesn't have to break you. Oftentimes, God will allow the breakup to position you for your purpose.

15

I KNEW YOU

"Before I shaped you in the womb, I knew all about you. Before
you saw the light of day, I had holy plans for you: A prophet to
the nations - that's what I had in mind for you."
Jeremiah 1:5 MSG

Every year on my birthday, my mother would recite the
story of when I was born. "On July 17th!" Although I am her
only audience, her joy radiates throughout the room. "Brittany,
my firstborn. God blessed me with a baby girl. 7lbs and 11oz,"
she always says with passion. "Beautiful slanted eyes, round
nose, curly black hair…"And she always ends with chuckles,
"and let's not forget a head shaped like her Daddy's."

As I have grown older, I realized how much I treasure my
mother's stories. For one, she is quite animated when she tells
it, acting, singing, and doing voice overs! I've always told her
that she should have performed on Broadway. But nonetheless,

each year she brings a different aspect to the story, always something I haven't heard before.

One year, she shared that while she was carrying me, she was involved in a bad car accident and feared she had lost me. But after a check-up at the doctor, she knew I would be okay. Or, the time when she was eight months pregnant with me and a prophet told her he saw that she was carrying a beautiful girl that would impact nations.

Oh the beauty of God knowing you before anyone else! Before you were born, He knew your every weakness and your every strength. Your likes and dislikes. Your successes and failures. He even knew your imperfections and qualities before you were on the earth. He knew your value and worth. He knew your visions and goals. Your talents and skills. Your power and resilience. God knows you better than anyone. Yes, our mothers carried us. Yes, we are the product of our Father's seed. But God is the master designer of our being. He fashioned us in His likeness and knows the very hairs on our heads. He knows everything about us. Even when it comes down to our purpose on this earth.

I am frequently asked, "Brittany, how do I know my purpose? In my understanding, I have found purpose to be as simple as this: a well-designed plan that was created specifically for you. Included in the plan are tools (your gifts), which are used to help you serve effectively in that purpose. Discovering your purpose is sometimes easier said than done. It is easy to say that God brought you into existence to fulfill His greater plan, but discovering what that plan looks like requires work. We have all pulled our hairs out, driven ourselves crazy figuring out what that well-designed plan looks like.

And, I am no exception. Just like you, I have asked God this question many times. Then he dropped this revelation bomb on me. Have you ever wondered why you are so passionate about a particular thing above anything else? Do you ever wonder why you love dancing, writing, singing, or acting? Or, why you enjoy serving or encouraging people? Or, why you love to solve problems, are so passionate about finances, law, or science? It's simple. When God created you, He didn't just breathe life into your body, but He also breathed your purpose in you. There's a reason why some things come naturally to you. The reason is simple, those are the gifts that He instilled in you to operate in your purpose.

I encourage you to discover and utilize those gifts to their fullest capacity. Do not let your gifts die. Do not let them wilt away. These tools (your gifts) will be used to help you operate efficiently and effectively in your purpose. I challenge you to use them now! Set aside time each day to perfect your gift. Whether you spend two to six hours a day rehearsing, drawing, writing, recording, blogging, vlogging, designing, or planning that business; God wants you to utilize your time wisely. When you focus on the preparation, the opportunity will soon be knocking at your door.

Let's recap! The more you seek God, the more He will reveal your purpose to you. And when He shows you, I know

He will guide you to the destiny in which He created you to be. God created you for a special purpose, to fulfill His will. I am a firm believer that you are chosen by God. I am a firm believer that your purpose is going to touch many lives and impact nations. I am a firm believer that time waits on no one. That we must utilize our time wisely and effectively.

PRAY ON PURPOSE

I AM fearfully and wonderfully made.

I AM the head and not the tail.

I AM above and not beneath.

I AM the lender and not the borrower.

I AM love, joy, and peace.

I AM a generational curse breaker.

I AM free.

I AM walking in my purpose.

In Jesus' name, Amen.

16

GET OFF THE BOAT

"But Jesus spoke to them at once. "Don't be afraid," he said. "Take courage. I am here!" Then Peter called to him, "Lord, if it's really you, tell me to come to you, walking on the water." "Yes, come," Jesus said. So Peter went over the side of the boat and walked on the water toward Jesus." Matthew 14:27-29 NLT

It was Fourth of July and we were heading to D.C. to celebrate the nation's birthday festivities. My brother LJ was driving, my best friend Hyedi was riding shotgun, and I was relaxing in the backseat of LJ's 2014 White Altima. We had the windows down, our Ray Ban shades on, and Lecrae's *I'm turnt* blasting in the background. You couldn't tell us anything, we knew D.C. was not ready for all this "swag."

As I write this story, I cannot help but laugh. Our two-hour car ride had become a two-hour concert with acoustics and us singing at the tops of our lungs. I had my head back on the headrest and all I could do was smile. I really needed this getaway and I was glad to be on it. As my two road trip mates continued to be each other's backup singer, I stuck my head outside the window and embraced the feeling of the fresh air rubbing against my face.

"Here's to a new start," I thought to myself. "No more drama, no more lies, and no more boyfriend." A few days before our trip, I found out that I was not his No. 1 as I had thought. Apparently, he was still involved with his previous girlfriend. I am sad to say that I knew it. You would think after so much experience in this area that I would have dropped him like it was hot and kept it moving. But, I didn't. Sometimes history can keep you bound.

When you have known someone for more than 10 years, it's not easy to let go. I couldn't tell anyone at the time, not even Hyedi or LJ. I was embarrassed and worried about what they would say. I was especially worried about Hyedi. She is my best friend and a strong black woman, and you know how fiercely loyal we are to our girlfriends. She would not be happy to hear about how he had treated me. So, I kept my pain a secret.

Have you ever held on to a secret pain that you were afraid to tell someone? The fact that he was with another woman hurt me to the depths of my soul. But, I kept my pain quiet for the sake of protecting him and the side woman. If my family knew he was messing around, I knew it would be the last of him, and us. So, no matter how much it hurt, I promised myself I would take my pain to my grave.

121

Arriving in D.C., we wasted no time. Our trip and all of that singing had left us hungry. We parked the car, checked into our hotel, and hopped on the metro heading to Chinatown for food. Our afternoon was lovely, full of jokes, laughs, and occasional brother-sister, best friend pettiness. After dinner, we joined the crowds of people migrating toward the National Mall to see D.C.'s annual fireworks show. People sported red, white and blue hats, t-shirts, shorts and dresses, ready to celebrate America's Independence. Unbeknownst to me, I was about to encounter an independence of my own. After the fireworks had ended, we quickly rushed to the metro to head back to our hotel. It felt like the longest ride of my life. I tried so hard to maintain the smile on my face and keep my composure, but I couldn't. Once we got back to our suite, I laid across the bed and hid my face in the pillow. It was as if the explosions in the sky opened up something inside of me.

"What's wrong hun?" Hyedi asked. LJ and Hyedi sat on the bed next to me and begin to rub my back. "Hey Britt, talk to us, what's bothering you?" LJ asked with concern. "Nothing guys," I said. "Just my first Independence Day alone...and without him...you know..."

They exchanged a quick side eye and smirk...nothing gets by these two. They were sensing something deeper and refused to back down. "Tell us the truth Britt." I lifted my head off the pillow and began to sob. "Am I not beautiful enough for him?" I was in so much pain that I could barely get the words out, all I could do was weep.

LJ lifted my head from the pillow and I looked over to Hyedi to see that she was crying too. I knew she understood and could relate to my pain all too well. Taking my hand, she wrapped it around her, while LJ took the other side and wrapped his arms around me. This was my release. For too long, I was afraid to express what I was feeling inside. Having the two of them with me was the best thing for my heart. I was tired of pretending that I was happy in this relationship. I was tired of pretending that we were the best couple. Truthfully, we were not. My heart was ready for a change and I was ready to embrace it.

After our heart-to-heart, LJ and Hyedi starting getting ready for bed, but I stayed up. I took out my phone and opened my Bible app. I began to search the scriptures to find an encouraging word of faith. The one that caught my attention was the story of Peter walking on water. I believe God had a reason for the story of Jesus and Peter walking on water.

Scripture describes, "After more than 5,000 souls were fed, Jesus sent His disciples ahead while He said goodbye. He instructed the disciples to get into their boat and sail to the other side of Galilee. As they left, Jesus went to the mountain top to pray" (Matthew 14:22-23 NIV). Scripture says, "Later that night, he was there alone, and the boat was already a considerable distance from land, buffeted by the waves because the wind was against it. Shortly before dawn Jesus went out to them, walking on the lake. When the disciples saw him walking on the lake, they were terrified. "It's a ghost," they said, and cried out in fear" (Matthew 14:23-26 NIV). Jesus came on the scene and told the disciples "to not be afraid" (Matthew 14:27 NIV). When Peter heard this, he said, "Lord, if it's you, tell me to come to you on the water" (Matthew 14:28 NIV). Jesus tells Peter to "Come." Without hesitation, Peter gets out the boat and begins to walk on water (Matthew 14:29 NIV).

Once I made the decision to fully walk in my purpose, I was often reminded of the story of Peter. He was criticized for not having enough faith to walk on water, but rarely do we focus on the behavior of the other disciples. Why did the rest of the disciples stay in the boat? I have read this story many times, but didn't grasp the revelation until recently. Here's four things God showed me:

1. *Relationships are a lot like the boat that Peter and the disciples were in.* Boats can either take you to your destiny or sail you away from it. In order to walk on water, Peter had to keep his focus on Jesus. When it comes to choosing relationships, we have to keep our focus on God first. As crazy and uneasy as this may sound, the majority of my relationships have taken me away from the will of God and the purpose for my life. Could I have prevented it? Yes. But I chose my own will and way, instead of His, and that resulted in a lot of tears, depression, and hurt. The Bible tells us, "In all your ways acknowledge Him, And He will direct your paths" (Proverbs 3:6 NKJV). When you seek God, He will give you His eyes and direct your heart. He will keep you away from the

counterfeits and prepare your heart for the perfect fit. Oftentimes, we mistake our emotions for God's will. Let's not get the two confused. God's will is not always soothing to your ears, but it is always a blessing to your heart. Let God lead you to the right boat.

2. *The people in the boat with you are a reflection of you and where you are going.* My mother always taught me to be careful about who I chose to have a relationship with. People can either be a *stumbling block* or a *stepping stone* to your destiny. My grandmother always says, "Birds of feather flock together." When I was young I would laugh at that saying. But now that I am older, I know it is so true. The people you choose to associate with will influence your life's direction. If you are moving forward, but the person you are with is not, I guarantee that he or she will eventually hold you back and impact your forward movement. One day, you will suddenly find yourself 10 steps behind when you should have been 20 steps ahead.

3. *When God calls you out of a relationship, he is calling you to step into a relationship with Him.* Jesus was calling Peter to step out of the boat away from the "destiny doubters" and the "faith killers." When you are surrounded by these type of individuals, it's hard to focus on God and your purpose. These types of people are assigned to keep you in the bondage of the boat. Since they are bound, they want to keep you bound too.

4. *Don't pay attention to the elements of the environment.* In other words, do not focus on distractions when it comes to your relationship with God. Distractions are used to get you off track from your purpose and out of the will of God. If you want to walk in your purpose, I urge you to keep your focus only on Him. When you start looking around at who is doing what and what is happening nearby, you will easily get distracted. When you begin to compare your position in life to others, you will lose sight of where you are supposed to be going. Remember, the race of purpose is "not to the swift" (Ecclesiastes 9:11 NKJV). Your purpose may not be someone else's. There were times where I took my focus off of God, and found myself drowning in my own mess. I was so consumed with comparing myself to others, that I forgot who I was. I often felt I wasn't good enough and thought I didn't have it like everyone else. Had I kept my eyes on God, I would have been further ahead.

I encourage you to use these revelations to bring clarity to your purpose. Study them, memorize them, and engrain them on your heart. Decide if you are going to be a Peter and step out of the boat on faith or be one of the other disciples and remain in the boat? I must say, walking out of a toxic relationship to fulfill my purpose was an act of courage. But once I got off the boat of uncertainty and pain, I was able to walk in freedom, I was liberated. As I walked toward my Father, I was reminded that He will never forsake me in a boat of my trial, nor will He ever let me fall as I walk towards Him in faith.

God wants us to walk in an unwavering faith when it comes to purpose. Sometimes God has to get us out of our comfort zone, get us off the boat, and to put our trust in Him. This is a reassuring lesson. God can help us get out of any situation. He did it for me and I am confident that He will do it for you.

PRAY ON PURPOSE

Dear God, give me the faith and courage to get off the boat. I do not want to be on a boat with "destiny doubters" and "faith killers." God, I pray that you will be my guide. For your thoughts are higher than my thoughts and your ways are higher than my ways. Teach me your way, O Lord. In Jesus' name, Amen.

17

SEASONS

"Rest in the Lord, and wait patiently for Him; Do not fret because of him who prospers in his way, Because of the man who brings wicked schemes to pass." Psalm 37:7 NKJV

It's 11 o'clock and Labor Day is approaching its final hour. The cookouts have died down, there is no more echo of children's voices in the streets. The kids are sound asleep now, ready for the new school year to start the next day. There is complete silence. But, I cannot sleep. My restless mind is racing, wondering... *what's next for my life?*

I'd been obedient to God's will by ending my relationship with a man who was no good for me. But, I was still struggling with how to start a relationship with my purpose. I'd regularly question God. *When will my time come? When will You remove me from the pit I'm in?* We are taught not to question God. We are taught to wait on the Lord. But let's be real, sometimes His silence can be agonizing.

What do you do when you find yourself in a silent season? What do you do when you keep asking God questions, but He gives you the silent treatment? What do you do when the next direction is not clear, when you feel stuck at a crossroads, and you fervently seek Him, but...He's just not answering?

We have all been in a place of feeling *stuck*. We've all found ourselves in between seasons and on the verge of giving up and throwing in the towel. We have all been in that place where we have made demands on God, saying things like, "If you don't move by the end of this week, I will make the decision myself!"

Silent seasons are often filled with many questions and thoughts. We think about the things that we have done. We rationalize with God. We say, "God, haven't I paid my tithes? God, haven't I prayed and fasted? God, haven't I been faithful?" At such times, we talk to God as if He has forgotten, as if He has no memory of our faithfulness and who we are. But God sees, hears, and knows. He is omniscient, He is an all-knowing God. Just because we don't understand the season, doesn't mean He has forgotten us. God is omnipresent, He is always there. Just because we are not always there with Him, doesn't mean He isn't always there for us.

Right now, I want you to take a moment and think about all the things God has done for you in your life. Even within the last month. Write down the situations and people He has delivered you from. Write down the things and situations He has blessed you with. If He was God in those seasons, don't you think He is the God of the right now in your waiting season?

We get angry and frustrated with God because we feel like He is not moving in our timing, that He is not moving as fast as we would like. We put Him on a time limit. But, when we do that, we are boxing Him in. We cannot put God in a box. We cannot expect God to move at our pace. God is the I AM. He is sovereign. So trust God, trust His process, and trust that what He has promised He shall fulfill and do.

Trust me. I know that waiting on God to direct you in your purpose is not easy. The Scripture says, in Proverbs, "Trust in the Lord with all your heart, And lean not on your own understanding; In all your ways acknowledge Him, And He shall direct your paths" (Proverbs 3:5-6 NKJV). Tell God how you feel. Write it out. Pray it out. Talk it out. Scream it out. He is listening. Do not allow the enemy to convince you that God is not there. Do not allow the enemy to make you feel that it's not worth waiting on God. Do not allow the enemy to make you feel like God is not going to move on your behalf. He wants His children to talk to Him. He wants His children to commune with Him. For He is a good father. Sooner or later, if you continue to walk faithfully in your purpose, the waiting on the Lord will turn in your complete favor.

PURPOSE IS CALLING

One evening, as I drove home from the gym I felt led to call my brother, LJ. I was approaching my 30th birthday and I needed advice on the pursuit of purpose. I could've called a number of people in my life, but something inside told me to reach out to my brother. "Hey LJ. I need your advice on purpose." I told him that I had this burning desire to write inspirational books, become a life coach, and impact people far and wide. The question was, how would I do it?

I explained that I'd carried this passion around with me since I was a little girl, but recently, it had grown much stronger. It was to the point where I would go to bed with it and wake up to it. I didn't talk to a lot of people about it, because I'd found that in the past, I would share ideas and dreams with people and they would knock them down. But, I knew I could trust LJ.

"How did you know the right time to move into your purpose?" I asked him. "God will first birth the desire in your spirit," he said. "Next, He will connect you to the *resources* for your purpose and begin to *prepare* you for the *opportunity*. While He is preparing you, He will *unlock* the *strategies* for your purpose. Then He will give you a sense of urgency to *pursue* it. That's when you know it's time to *execute*." He continued to explain that God was trying to get my attention because there were people out there that I needed to reach. *When God gives you that urgency Brittany, there is a mandate that you need to fulfill immediately.*

Scripture says, "You can make many plans, but the Lord's purpose will prevail" (Proverbs 19:21 NLT). I found that scripture to be so relevant to my situation. I have been carrying these gifts around for a long time. In fact, God was showing me that I was sitting on my gifts and that the time to use them was well overdue. I knew it was time to lay aside every weight and birth this vision I had for my life. I didn't want to abort it as I had so many other times. This time, I was determined to run with the vision God had instilled in me.

Before we ended our conversation, he spoke of positioning myself for my purpose. "God will begin to set you aside from the crowd," he said. As he spoke, I could feel chills run through my body. I knew God was using LJ to speak to me. God had divinely placed me in a "shifting season." I can recall several occasions where God separated me from so many people. People that I once called friends, people that I thought cared for my well-being, just slowly drifted away. At the time, I didn't understand it. I was too focused on questioning what I'd done rather than letting God be God.

Now I know that God was positioning me to be underneath His care for my life. He was positioning me to write this book. Before the "shifting season," I had so many distractions that I was unable to focus on the book. This time, God had me to Himself. He had me in a place where He could download His inspiration and allow His Holy Spirit to minister through me.

This period of my life taught me to walk in the "I Will." Every day I would look in the mirror and say, "I will finish this book. I will be an author. I will be a purpose coach. I will pursue my dreams." I was determined that I will follow through with the purpose that God destined for my life. In order to step into the calling God created for me, I had to change my mindset. I had to be confident and assured in my "I Will" affirmations. Remember, death and life are in the power of the tongue (Proverbs 18:21 KJV). How do you expect God to take you higher when you are not confident in who you are and whose you are?

I never knew that this would be the last conversation I would have with my brother about purpose. He would pass away only a short time later. His words changed my very outlook on how I saw my life and the purpose God had for me. You may be asking yourself about your own gifts and your own purpose. Like me, God has placed many gifts and a purpose inside of you too. And now is the time to step out. Purpose has been ringing your phone and leaving voicemails for a long time. It's time to answer the call.

KNOCK, KNOCK! WHO'S THERE?

Knock, knock! Who's there? The *new you*. Yes, God wants to show you a new version of yourself. No longer does He want you to feel inadequate or invaluable. No longer does He want you to feel that you are incapable of achieving your dreams and goals. Scripture says, "Ask and it will be given to you; seek and you will find; knock and the door will be opened to you" (Matthew 7:7 NIV). It's time to put an end to the misconception of yourself. It is time to turn away from all the naysayers and dream slayers.

For so long, you have walked in defeat. For so long, you have walked in the guilt of your past. It's time to embark on a new journey and start walking in the power of the I AM. God is positioning you and preparing you for a destiny that has only your name on it. Do not ignore this knock. Answer it, open the door and welcome the newness that God is bringing to your life.

Knock, knock! Who's there? *Confidence*. God is giving you an unwavering confidence and a strong backbone. He is also giving you an abundance of faith, courage, wisdom, resilience, and toughness to conquer that which He has for you. There are so many doors that God is about to open for your life and you cannot walk through them if you carry the bags of uncertainty and weakness with you. Do not ignore this knock! Open the door and welcome in the resources that He is offering to you that will help launch you into your destiny.

Knock, knock! Who's there? *Multiplication*. Get ready for a season of multiplication. God is going to multiply every area of your life. Even the areas that you have lacked in will multiply triple-fold. You have endured so much hardship from the time you were born. You have fought battles that should have taken you out. But what you have lost, God is going to replenish in you. He is going to fill you up with everything you need for your destiny. Do not ignore this knock! Open the door and welcome in the abundance God has for you and your purpose.

DO NOT REVERSE YOUR RECOVERY

Before we move into the next section, I want you to think about this question. When is the last time, that after a breakup, you gave yourself enough time to truly heal? It is very common these days to see a person end one relationship and quickly jump into another relationship within weeks. You might think this does not apply to you because the person you were seeing was "technically not my boyfriend or my girlfriend."

But, let's be clear. A relationship is best described as a connection, association, or involvement between persons. So, just because you have not given that person an "official" title, does not negate the fact that you are either emotionally *connected,* physically *associated,* or sexually *involved* with them.

We allow society to make us think that "waiting" is old school. But the truth is, it is one of the greatest gifts you can give yourself. Why? Because when we are in the waiting process:

1) We are growing in our relationship with God.
2) We are healing and building ourselves.
3) We are finding and pursuing our purpose.

However, the pressures of this world can take us away from the will of God. The world will program us to think that pursuing a relationship is the prescription to our loneliness. When in fact, that pursuit is just a cover-up for our brokenness.

As I explained in previous chapters, what you don't heal will eventually kill. If you don't heal your brokenness, it will eventually kill your growth to wholeness. If you don't heal your insecurities, they will eventually kill your self-confidence. If you don't heal your lust, it will kill the true love God has for you. If you don't heal your anger, it will eventually kill your peace. So, let God be your Healer today! Do not wrap your heart around relationships just to fill a void. Let God fill the void. Do not seek your recovery through any relationship or situationship. Seek your recovery through a relationship with God.

It's important to note that when you seek your recovery through a relationship with God, you give Him full access to heal your mind, body, heart, and soul. As you are healed in these areas, you can operate effectively and efficiently in your life. However, be careful of trying to short-hand the healing process. You will damage yourself the more when you continue to date while you are healing. We can be single for weeks or even a few months, and then suddenly catch "dry phone or social media fever."

For instance, every time we see an engagement or marriage post, our biological clock starts ticking louder than before. We can be doing so well in our recovery, and then we let the pressures of *who is doing what,* make us fall into a relationship relapse. The next thing you know, you are calling your ex or that "friend with benefits" to fill that void. Pump the brakes!

We are so desperate to be in a "situationship," so desperate to avoid loneliness, that we neglect the very thing God is trying to do with us, through us, and for us.

Do not reverse your recovery. Do not go back to the past. If God has brought you out, then stay out. If He has closed a door, don't go knocking on it asking to get back in. God sees down the road and around the corner. In other words, He sees what we don't see. He knows the traps of the enemy. He knows what is good for you and what can easily destroy you. If God says, "No," then accept His will for your life.

As we close this chapter, remember that the journey to healing still continues. I am a firm believer that we should work to see our circumstances on a spiritual level rather than just looking at the surface. If you don't allow yourself to heal fully, you cannot operate in your purpose effectively and efficiently. If you don't allow yourself to heal fully, you will repeat what you did not repair. Scripture says, "You were running superbly! Who cut in on you, deflecting you from the true course of obedience" (Galatians 5:7 MSG).

I challenge you to not reverse your recovery, but to pursue your purpose with full speed. God's purpose for your life is waiting for you. There are so many broken people that need to be touched by the ministry of your purpose. I believe you are one step closer to entering into the blessings God has for you.

Daughters and sons, the time is now to answer the call of purpose and to open the door to your destiny. Yes, there will be naysayers, destiny doubters, and faith killers who will attempt to hinder your healing process. But stand firm on your *FL;P* foundation. If God is for you, who can be against you? (Romans 8:31 KJV). I pray that you propel into *Finding Love In Purpose*, by taking your purpose by the hand, grip it tight, and walk forward never looking back. It's forward movement and thinking from here, anything less must go!

I salute you for your courage to travel this journey with me. Now that you have the tools to *Finding Love In Purpose*, may the Lord keep you, establish you, and perfect you into the purpose driven man and woman He has created you to be!

PRAY ON PURPOSE

For so long, God has been knocking on the door of your heart. But because you have built so many walls around your heart, you refuse to allow anyone to come in, even the Father. I pray that you welcome the Great I Am into your life.

Heavenly Father, I am ready to launch into my destiny. I will cast down my nets and trust that your perfect will is what's best for me. Teach me to stay on the path to recovery.

Teach me to remain in position to receive complete healing and restoration. I desire to be healed in my heart, mind, body, and soul.

Guard my eyes and allow me to see what you see. Allow me to see on the spiritual level and not on the surface level. Guard my heart and allow me to heal properly. Do not allow me to reverse my recovery. I take authority over my recovery. I shall wait on the Lord and be of good courage. I shall listen to the voice of God and not subject myself to the voice of my past. In Jesus' name, Amen.

S.E.E.

SELF EVALUATION EXERCISES

PART I: F.I.N.D.

Chapter 1: Change Your Anthem
1. What are the negative anthems that you continue to sing?
2. Write your life anthem. What does it sound like?

Chapter 2: Finding The Word
1. Describe a time where you lost your worth for the sake of making it work.
2. Describe a time in your life that God performed a search and rescue.

Chapter 3: Finding Your Power
1. Describe a time where you gave your "last" for the sake of saving the relationship. How did it make you feel?
2. Describe a time where you found your power. What were the steps you took?

Chapter 4: Finding Your Strength
1. Describe a time where God took you through spiritual strength training.
2. Describe a time when you were dishonest to your purpose. How did it make you feel?

Chapter 5: Finding The Will
1. Identify the addiction(s) in your life that are hindering you from reaching your purpose.
2. Why do we refuse to let go of the person God has commanded us to let go of?

PART II: L.O.V.E.

Chapter 6: Why Did You Shape Me This Way?
1. What are some things you highlight negatively about yourself?
2. What are some words you can use to counteract those negative thoughts about yourself?

Chapter 7: Confessions From The Bayou
1. Have you been afraid to share the grace of God (your testimony) with others? What held you back?
2. Have you worn masks for the sake of covering up what you're battling with on the inside?

Chapter 8: To Love Me or Not To Love Me? That Is The Question
1. Describe a time where God had to get your attention because you were off track.
2. What did you look like *before* the counterfeit relationship?
3. What did you look like *after* the counterfeit relationship?

Chapter 9: What's Makes You Happy?
1. When was the last time you were truly happy?
2. What does being happy look like? List 3-5 examples.

Chapter 10: Table For One, Please!
1. How do you get to learn you?
2. What are steps you can take to start loving yourself?

PART III: I.N.

Chapter 11: Well-ness Check
1. Have you become comfortable in captivity? If so, explain why?
2. When is the last time you had a well-ness check?

Chapter 12: Residue
1. Think of a time when your ex showed up at an event. How did you react?
2. Have you negotiated your purpose for the sake of having one last night with the counterfeit person?

Chapter 13: Beauty for Ashes
1. Have you ever felt like you did not deserve God's grace? Why did you feel that way?
2. What is harder to forgive: yourself or others? Why?

Chapter 14: Obedience Is Better Than Sacrifice
1. How did you operate in sacrifice?
2. What are some ways you can walk in His obedience?

PART IV: P.U.R.P.O.S.E.

Chapter 15: I Knew You
1. Write down 3-5 inspiring declarations about yourself.
2. Share why did you choose these declarations and how will you apply them to your life?

Chapter 16: Get Off The Boat
1. Who are the "destiny doubters" and the "faith killers" in your life? How will you separate yourself from these individuals?
2. Will you be a Peter (get out the boat) or will you be like the other disciples (stay in the boat)?

Chapter 17: Seasons
1. Have you questioned the timing of God? Give examples.
2. Describe a time when you experienced a silent season.
3. Are you confident in who you are and whose you are? Explain why.
4. Can you recall a time when your purpose was calling you? How did you respond?
5. What gift is burning on the inside that you want to pursue?
6. What has prevented you from launching your gift? How can you overcome that?
7. When was the last time you gave yourself time to heal? Did you allow the healing to manifest completely?
8. Who did you allow to hinder your recovery? Was it worth going back?

ACKNOWLEDGEMENTS

"I have not stopped thanking God for you. I pray for you constantly." Ephesians 1:16 NLT

First and foremost, I would like to thank God. Without you, this book would not be possible. God, thank you for being the mastermind of this book. Thank you for teaching me to step out on faith and not fear. You have carried me through every storm and have caught every tear. You have been my strength when I was weak and when I felt like I couldn't make it. You remind me every day that you validate my future and not man. Thank you for being the Way, the Truth, and the Life in my purpose. Your Word has helped me through some of the toughest times. God, thank you for helping me to find love in purpose. Thank you for your divine connection, provision, and favor you have bestowed upon me in this journey. God, I give you all the honor and praise. For all glory belongs to your Name.

I would like to honor my amazing parents, Lowell Sr. and Robin Brooks for their never-ending support. Truly, you have been the pillars in my life since the beginning. As much as I wanted to give up, you always pushed me to go forward. Thank you for being the sound wisdom to my ears. Thank you for listening to my stories and giving your input as I was carrying out the vision in private before it was public. Thank you for teaching me how to build my foundation in Christ. Thank you for being examples of how to press through every storm and to not give up on my purpose. Thank you for showing me what it means to be "Changed" and "Not Chained." I love you both with all my heart and I am beyond blessed to have wonderful parents such as you.

To my brother Gabriel Brooks, you are truly a messenger from God. I am in awe of your wisdom and how it has guided me throughout this whole journey. Thank you for pushing me to lead my own vision and to stick with the vision. Thank you for the daily phone calls to make sure I completed my goals. Thank you for attending my impromptu reading and listening sessions and providing your sound wisdom. Thank you for picking me up when I wavered in fear and doubt. I love you with all my heart and I thank you for always being there for me. You believed in my vision, my dreams, my purpose, since day one. Gabriel, I admire and thank you for your unwavering faith. You have taught me so much about myself and I will hold dear to that. You will forever be my heartbeat, my joy, my smile, my love.

To my daily inspiration and purpose partner, Bradley Jones. You are truly an amazing person (inside and out) and I am so blessed to do purpose with you. From the depths of my heart, thank you for reading chapter after chapter. Thank you for listening to my stories during the late nights and the early mornings. Thank you for capturing the vision of this book. Your steadfast faith and unwavering support has played a huge part in the completion and success of this book. For it has taught me to never give up, to trust God, and to pursue my purpose with full speed. I thank God for the favor upon your life, for it has connected me to some amazing people. In all, thank you for truly being by my side. Thank you for being a great support to my family and I. I love you dearly.

To my dearest best friend and sister, Hyedi Branch. When I first shared the vision of the book and what I desired to do in my life, you didn't question it, but told me to "Pursue!" Thank you for teaching me how to live for me and not for others. Thank you for encouraging me to move forward in my purpose and to not look back. Thank you for listening to my book ideas and providing your sound advice. Thank you for consistently being there for my family and I after the passing of my brother, LJ. We have shared many tears, while writing this book. You have been my cheerleader and have kept me lifted through some difficult times. You are the most transparent, loving, and caring person I know. I love you girl.

Immeasurable appreciation to my editor, Kellie Tabron, for her unwavering support, commitment, and mentorship throughout this book process. You are truly the midwife of this book – your help in strengthening my ideas and bringing them to life was invaluable. God truly answered my prayers when He divinely connected our paths. I am eternally grateful for your untiring dedication and being a source of motivation. God bless you.

I humbly extend my thanks to my loving grandmother, Jerrie Shirley Young; my late grandfather, Robert Henry Young, Sr.; spiritual advisors Pastor Sherman and Dr. Sharon Spratley; and to a host of confidantes, counselors, mentors, colleagues, family, and friends. Thank you for your support, encouragement, and continued prayers throughout my life. I love you and may God continue to bless you.

With Love,

Brittany Nicole Brooks

Made in the USA
San Bernardino, CA
23 November 2018